CONTACT

OF THE 5TH KIND

Philip J. Imbrogno
Marianne Horrigan

1997
Llewellyn Publications
St. Paul, Minnesota, USA 55164-0383

FIRST EDITION
First Printing, 1997

Cover design by Tom Grewe
Editing and layout by Marguerite Krause
Project management and design by Connie Hill
Photos by Philip J. Imbrogno

Library of Congress Cataloging-in-Publication Data
Imbrogno, Philip.
        Contact of the 5th kind : the silent invasion has begun—what the government has covered up / Philip Imbrogno, Marianne Horrigan
             p.   cm. —)
        Includes index.
        ISBN 1-56718-361–1 (trade pbk.)
     1. Human-alien encounters.   2. Unidentified flying objects.
3. Civilization—Extraterrestrial influences   I. Horrigan, Marianne.
II. Title.
BF2050.I44   1997
001.942—dc21   97-22260

Llewellyn Publications
A Division of Llewellyn Worldwide, Ltd.
St. Paul, Minnesota 55164-0383, U.S.A.

George and Maria have a daughter who is almost two years old. One day she brought out her doll and asked her Mom to open its head.

Maria asked her where she had seen something like that and the little girl told her mother, "They do it to daddy at night."

Chilling, isn't it? And it's only one small piece of the compelling evidence of alien contact you'll find in these pages. *Contact of the 5th Kind* presents dozens of cases that uncover the real truth about our contacts with a non-human intelligence that may not be extraterrestrial, but *interdimensional*.

Contact of the 5th Kind will shake the toughest skeptics and confirm all of our deepest fears about government conspiracy—and the aliens who have infiltrated our cities, our countries, our entire world.

Read the evidence, then decide for yourself:

- Hard proof for contacts of the fifth kind, where humans psychically encounter or channel alien intelligences
- Abductee and contactee testimony…the link between blood type and alien contact…and eyewitness reactions to seeing UFOs
- Convincing eyewitness testimony of government cooperation with alien intelligences—and government efforts to "fake" a UFO
- Disturbing evidence that alien-human babies exist
- "High strangeness": cases that include strange sounds, electromagnetic phenomena, and psychological and physical effects on humans
- Statistical analysis pinpointing the center of UFO activity—in the state of New York
- Interviews with contactees who continue to channel extraterrestrial intelligences after their alien encounters

About the Author

Philip J. Imbrogno has been a science educator for the past fifteen years, currently teaching at a school in New York state. He was coauthor, with the late Dr. J. Allen Hynek, of the book *Night Siege: The Hudson Valley UFO Sightings* (Ballantine Books, 1987), and also wrote *Crosswalks Across the Universe: A Guide to Astronomy* (Viking Press, 1982). He has appeared on or provided research for the Geraldo, Regis and Kathy Live, and Oprah television shows, and his work has appeared in *The New York Times, The New York Daily News, The San Francisco Chronicle, Scientific American, Spotlight, UFO Universe, FATE,* and *Unexplained Universe.* He writes an astronomy column in the *Southern Connecticut Newspaper*, and is a member of the board of directors of the Bowman Observatory in Greenwich, Connecticut.

To Write to the Author

If you wish to contact the author or would like more information about this book, please write to the author in care of Llewellyn Worldwide, and we will forward your request. Both the author and publisher appreciate hearing from you and learning of your enjoyment of this book and how it has helped you. Llewellyn Worldwide cannot guarantee that every letter written to the author can be answered, but all will be forwarded. Please write to:

Llewellyn's New Worlds of Mind and Spirit
P.O. Box 64383, Dept. K361–1,
St. Paul, MN 55164-0383, U.S.A.

Please enclose a self-addressed, stamped envelope for reply,
or $1.00 to cover costs.
If outside the U.S.A., enclose international postal reply coupon.

To Paul:

Always remember, "Can Do!"

Acknowledgments

We wish to thank the following organizations for their help during our research: The Mutual UFO Network, The Center for UFO Studies, SOPES in Belgium, and, finally, Citizens Against UFO Secrecy. We would also like to thank the following individuals for their assistance during our investigation: Chris Clark, John White, Karen Williams, Dennis Sant, Dean Fagerstrom, Scott and Loretta Chaney, and the many people who had a contact experience and told their story to us. We would also like to give special thanks to Fred Dennis, without whose sound advice and assistance this book would not have been possible.

Table Of Contents

Plates and Charts

CHAPTER ONE ...

INTRODUCTION

Something amazing is now taking place in the northeastern section of the United States. Since 1982, thousands of people say that they have had encounters with an object that was not of this earth. The object was reported to have been a UFO of gigantic proportions, larger than a football field. It hovered so close to the ground that many observers saw a dark gray superstructure connecting a series of multicolored lights. The UFO hovered over major highways in the area, causing traffic to come to a grinding halt. It was reported by people from all walks of life—doctors, pilots, scientists, and police officers, to name a few. The Federal Aviation Administration (FAA) tried to explain the sightings as merely ultralight planes flying in formation, helicopters, or even a blimp. It was clear, however, that the FAA's position provided no explanation for what the object actually was and where it came from.

1

The UFO became known as the "Hudson Valley UFO" since most of the reports from 1982 through 1984 came from the Hudson River Valley, just a few miles north of New York City. We learned that the UFO had been seen over most of the east coast of the United States, but most people never heard about those sightings.

On July 24, 1984 at 10:20 P.M., the object was video-taped by Robert Pozzouli, a family man and vice-president of a major electronics company in Brewster, New York. In the opinion of UFO skeptic Phil Klass, Pozzouli's videotape is perhaps the best nighttime image of a UFO on record. A former editor for *Aviation Weekly* suggests that the lights represent nothing more than lightweight aircraft flying in formation—a formation so close that the pilots would have to be flying with only six small inches between wing tip and wing tip.

We had the videotape sent to Dr. Lew Allen at the Jet Propulsion Laboratory in Pasadena, California. We wanted to know if the lights represented one solid object, or individual objects in formation. The tape was examined by some of the top imaging scientists in the country. Dr. Allen and the scientists of his imaging team stated that they believed that the lights represented one solid object, not separate objects. This would rule out the notion that the lights were planes. UFO skeptics cannot agree on what is causing the rash of UFO sightings, but the witnesses are sure of what they saw—something not from this planet.

The Hudson Valley sightings are documented in *Night Siege: The Hudson Valley UFO Sightings* (Ballantine Books 1987; *Night Siege 2nd Edition* to be released by Llewellyn Publications in April 1998), written by Phil Imbrogno, the

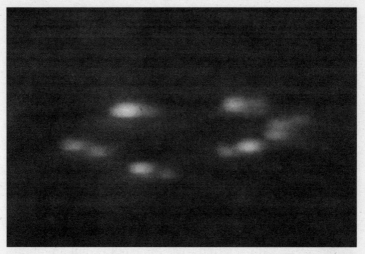

Plate 1. The Hudson Valley UFO. From a video taken on July 24, 1984, at about 10:30 P.M. in Brewster, New York. Despite analysis by the Jet Propulsion Laboratory, the lights remain unidentified.

late Dr. J. Allen Hynek, and Bob Pratt. However, another story remains to be told, a story so strange that we would have considered it pure science fiction if we had not researched it ourselves.

UFO sightings are on the rise across the country. The highest concentration seems to occur on the east coast of the United States. The greatest number of reports come from the New England area. These sightings are more than just reports of lights in the sky. Many of the observers report a further dimension to their experience. They feel they have made contact with an intelligence from another world—a Close Encounter of the Fifth Kind.

Technically speaking, a close encounter (CE) consists of seeing a UFO at very close range. UFO investigators, also known as Ufologists, have divided close encounter cases into four categories; we have added a fifth.

CE I: A sighting of a UFO at close range (within 600 feet).

CE II: A sighting at close range in which the UFO leaves some physical trace. The most common physical traces are burns in the ground, depressions in the ground, crushed vegetation and broken tree limbs, and, in rare cases, residue on the grass or ground that may resemble oil or fine powder.

CE III: A sighting in which the witnesses see one or more creatures or beings outside a landed UFO. In some cases the beings communicate with the witnesses. The beings are technically referred to as humanoids, but are popularly called ETs, aliens, and visitors.

CE IV: A sighting in which a person is abducted against his or her will (in most cases) by the intelligence from the UFO. Such cases are commonly known as Close Encounters of the Fourth Kind.

CE V: Contact between a human being and an intelligence not of this world. In some cases a UFO is seen; however, in other cases no UFO is reported.

Close encounter cases involve more than people reporting strange lights in the sky. Many people who have had a close encounter feel a personal connection with the UFO and the intelligence behind it. These people also feel that their encounter was no accident, but planned. During our investigation into close encounters, it became clear that any CE case represented some type of contact with the intelligence behind the UFO phenomenon.

On January 9, 1986 a giant UFO was reported over the skies in the greater Hartford, Connecticut area. At about 9:00 P.M., the police in the city of Hartford and neighboring towns started to receive dozens of calls concerning a low-flying object that displayed many bright lights. At first, the police dismissed the calls, but they grew concerned when the reports continued. By 9:15 the police telephone lines were jammed by calls from people reporting the object. At that time Hartford police were sent to investigate. As they approached Interstate Highway 84 in Hartford, they could see that traffic was backed up. They noticed that many motorists were getting out of their cars and looking up at the sky. The officers arrived just in time to see a large boomerang-shaped pattern of lights slowly drift toward the southeast.

Silent Approach

One witness who saw the UFO at that time was Mrs. Diane Duont, a 40-year-old resident of West Hartford. Mrs. Duont was driving in the area where I-84 runs into I-91, right in the heart of Hartford. Mrs. Duont recounted her sighting to us in the following words:

"I was driving north on 84 through the Hartford area. I was heading toward the I-91 turn-off when I noticed a formation of brilliant white lights approaching from the east. I thought that it looked quite unusual, and although I have seen large aircraft fly low over this area, I thought that this was unusually large.

"It continued to approach, and I thought at first that it was a large jet going to crash into the city. I pulled over to an exit, stopped the car, and got out. I looked back toward the highway because I heard the sound of brakes squealing. The cars along the highway had slowed down; some even stopped. This was dangerous, since this part of the highway is hectic and even under normal circumstances there are accidents all the time.

"I watched as these lights approached and I was surprised that I heard no sound at all. The lights seemed to be in a boomerang shape, and at this time all white. As it continued to approach I noticed red, blue, and green lights in between and very close to the white lights. The object then passed directly over my car, and as I looked up I saw a dark mass against the brighter night sky. I could not see any structure; I only saw a silhouette, but this thing blocked out the entire sky overhead.

"I estimated its size to be about that of a 747, but its shape was strange…it looked like a flying wing. The object then continued to move south. At this time it stopped and hovered for fifteen seconds, then continued to the southwest. It was a fantastic sight, and no matter how much you tell yourself that these things can't be real, I could find no answer as to what that thing could have been. It was not of this world!"

Most of the reports from that area all confirm that the UFO was very large, silent, and low. Most of the estimates place it about 500 to 800 feet above the ground. Bradley International Airport is close by, so how could an object this large have come into a populated area and remain undetected by radar? Local police were baffled by the sightings. Within twenty-four hours, Connecticut State Police issued a statement to all local law enforcement agencies and the media, in which they explained that the sightings were caused by nothing more than a group of stunt planes flying in formation. The FAA at Bradley would not confirm or deny that they had anything on radar, but insisted that the entire sighting over the Hartford area was a hoax created by a hot air balloon sent aloft. However, many people who saw the UFO that night say that these explanations don't fit. As one witness, a building inspector in Hartford, put it: "This thing about the UFO being aircraft or a balloon is a lot of crap."

The UFO did not disappear. Instead, it continued to head south and was seen over New Britain, Connecticut. There, many people ran out of their homes in time to watch the giant UFO pass overhead. The time was about 9:15 PM. One witness told us that he stood and watched it pass over the street he lives on. He reported that he saw the underside of the object, and it was a very dark gray. He also noticed all kinds of tubes and grids across the bottom. He said that the lights were flashing and were all white, except for one red one in the middle. The lights were arranged in a boomerang shape, but he could also see a dark structure that extended toward the rear that made the object appear kite-shaped. He and his neighbor just stood in awe as it passed over their row of homes without making a sound.

The UFO was seen heading northwest. At about 9:30 P.M. it was reported over Torrington, Connecticut, about fifteen miles west of Hartford. At this time dozens of calls were made to police headquarters in Torrington. Scores of calls were also made to local radio station WSNG.

One woman who lives in the greater Torrington area told police that she looked out the window and saw bright lights very low in the sky, approaching her home. At first she thought the lights belonged to an airplane about to crash. Frantically, she alerted her husband and three teenage children. The entire family watched the UFO get closer and closer.

The UFO continued to approach their home, moving very slowly. All they could see were approximately ten very bright, white lights. As they watched, the lights began to drop in altitude at a very quick rate, causing the family members to panic. The UFO hovered directly over their home, no more than 200 feet above the roof, and engulfed the entire house in a brilliant white light. The whole family ran into the house and down to the basement for shelter. They were certain that this object was not a plane or anything from this earth.

From the basement window they could still see the light. After several minutes the light went off. They then heard a rumbling sound that shook the entire house. After several minutes they ventured out of the basement, went outdoors, and scanned the skies, only to find the UFO gone.

The sighting was confirmed by several area residents in the sparsely populated area in which they live. The object was then seen heading toward downtown Torrington. Shortly afterward, the Torrington police received a deluge of calls reporting the UFO. The police, however, could do nothing, not even calm the people by explaining what was being seen.

Multiple Reports

The scenario described above has become a familiar event, one that has been repeated again and again. In 1984, a similar UFO flew over the towns of New Castle, Yorktown, and

Mount Kisco in Westchester County, New York, about fifty miles southeast of Torrington. Local police in these New York towns were helpless and could only stand in amazement as they observed an object reported to have been the size of a football field. As New Castle police Lieutenant Herbert Peterson put it, "If this thing can come here and do this, I want to know where the hell are our country's defenses?" Hartford and Torrington police were now experiencing the same frustration their colleagues in Westchester had experienced several years earlier. Federal spokesmen and state police provided theoretical explanations for the 1984 events, but no real answers.

As the UFO continued to move west, it was witnessed by an amazed Arnold Sprinster, his wife, and their friends. Their sighting took place near Whist pond, just off Route 4, about ten miles west of Torrington. Mr. Sprinster called us on January 11, 1986, just two days after the sighting. He was still quite excited about what he saw. Here is his sighting account:

"As we were approaching the pond area, I noticed a series of very bright white lights coming from the south. I called the lights to everyone's attention, at which point my friend said that it looked like a squadron of helicopters. The lights continued to approach very slowly. I stopped the car and rolled down the window to try to listen for some type of sound that could help me identify what the lights were. Off to my right was the pond; it was frozen at the time. We looked at the lights, and I knew that this was something strange. I told them it had to be a UFO, because it was large and there was no sound at all. My wife told me not to be silly. She thought I was fooling around, but I was dead serious.

"As it continued to approach, I could see a group of red lights mixed in with the white. I became very concerned, because this thing was still headed straight for us. I would estimate its altitude to have been no more than 500 feet. My friend's wife then said, "What the hell is it?" At this time the object was almost directly over the car and there was still no sound.

"The UFO started to drop lower as it continued to approach the car. I knew that no aircraft could possibly keep that altitude and go that slowly; plus, it was dead quiet. I opened the door and got out of the car. It was huge. It seemed like it took a long time to pass over us. At this point everyone started to get a little worried. I mean, here we were on this road with no other traffic. It could easily have done whatever it wanted to do with us. I looked up at the object as it was directly overhead. It was about 200 feet above the car. At that point all the white lights went out and I saw ten red lights, very small, surrounding a triangular-shaped object. The underside had one red light in the middle that illuminated part of the bottom. This was no UFO, it was a huge ship of some sort. It looked just like one of those spaceships in the science fiction movies, but this was real! The lights made it look even more weird. When the object was approaching, the white lights made it look like a boomerang in shape, but now, with the white lights off and the object directly overhead, it looked like a large triangle. When it passed overhead I looked up and saw this structure. There were parts that looked like they were soldered together, but very smoothly. It was made up of some kind of dark greyish material that had a very low reflectability.

"This was not any type of aircraft. I have an engineering background and have flown all kinds of small aircraft, and I know there is no way this was anything man-made. I saw this large object black out the entire sky as it passed over the car. It was easily the size of a football field.

"I also noticed that the underside was criss-crossed by a network of tubes and grill-like work. It looked like some sort of modern art. Then, without a sound, the red light in the middle of this thing detached itself and flew ahead of the object at a much greater speed. The red light circled the object three times, then went back to its original position in the middle of the underside. It just re-attached itself to the same place. By this time the UFO—or whatever it was—had passed over the car and made a very sharp turn toward the south. My wife and friends were yelling for us to get out of there, and I just stood outside the car and watched the thing until I lost it behind some trees.

"The entire sighting was about ten minutes long. The next day the papers carried a story stating that hundreds of people had seen it. The papers quoted a spokesman from Bradley International Airport, who said that the whole thing was a hoax created by five small aircraft in a tight formation. I saw this thing with friends and my wife, and I can tell you this was no plane! My wife never believed in UFOs, but after that night we are convinced that these things are real!"

At 9:45 P.M., the UFO was seen fifteen miles south of Torrington in the vicinity of the small Connecticut town of Thomaston. Torrington and Thomaston are connected by Route 8, a major highway in central Connecticut. At that time there were several reports from motorists in the area who saw the huge object drift overhead, moving in a southerly direction. Closer to Thomaston, along Route 8, several people stopped their cars and got out to watch the strange object pass above them. The Thomaston Police Department said it received several calls reporting an elliptical formation of white lights. It seemed that the UFO turned on more lights as it approached the Thomaston area. It now closely resembled the object that was caught on videotape by Robert Pozzouli on July 24, 1984 in Brewster, New York. Moments after the UFO was reported to them, Thomaston police received a call from the Connecticut State Police telling them that the lights were nothing more than a formation of planes from Hudson, New York. When this information came to our attention it puzzled us, since there are no real airports in that area, just two small landing fields. Furthermore, residents who saw the UFO over Thomaston were not convinced that airplanes were the answer to the mystery.

One person who did not accept the plane explanation was Paul Tracey of Thomaston. Tracy observed the UFO as it hovered above his home. "It was big and moved slowly," he said. "It made no noise, and that's what bugged me the most."

David Marcoux and his wife were driving home from downtown Thomaston when they also saw the UFO. "I thought at first it was a plane. It had rows of seven bright red lights, with a big red one that looked like a bright beacon in the middle."

When they got home, Mrs. Marcoux went inside to get a camera. The lights were far away by the time she returned but she still snapped off twenty frames, but none of them came out. Marcoux summed up his feelings about the sightings this way: "I would sure like to know what's going on."

Marcoux's feelings are echoed by the thousands living in the Hudson Valley of New York who saw the UFO from 1982 to 1984. As one witness told reporters, "We want answers, not explanations!"

A Power Surge?

Stranger still, two days later the lights were once again reported in the Thomaston area. On Monday, January 13, at about 10:30 P.M., a large number of people saw what they thought was an object the size of a football field that moved slowly and hovered at times. Most of the reports came from less populated regions, but only in the Thomaston area. Why did the UFO come back, and why only in the Thomaston area? So far as we know, there were no other reports from the surrounding towns that night.

If that wasn't strange enough, a more baffling occurrence took place the next day. When the people of Thomaston woke up Tuesday morning, they noticed that all of the electric clocks in the town had gained ten minutes. Middle school principal Douglas Harlow arrived at his office that morning to find that all of the school's clocks were ten minutes fast. "I couldn't figure it out," Harlow said.

Harlow was not the only one who could not figure it out. A spokesman for the Connecticut Light and Power Company speculated that sometime in the night a power surge somehow caused the clocks to move ahead. Philip Gervais, a shift supervisor for the utility, said that he had never heard of such a thing happening because of a power surge, but could find no other explanation. He did say that, although they had no report of a power surge the night before, there was a power loss in the area of Hummiston Court, where 109 homes went without electricity for several hours. The cause of the blackout was never determined, but the power company speculates that it was due to an over-loaded transformer. The blackout occurred very close to the area in which the UFO was seen, although no reports came from that particular street.

Whatever caused the clocks to speed up and the power to fail may never be known for sure. Many people speculated that the fast clocks had something to do with the sightings of the UFO the previous night and several days before. We know that UFOs have caused such electromagnetic effects as power surges and power blackouts, but was it responsible in this case? Whatever caused the clocks of Thomaston to speed ahead caused enough trouble to upset the morning routines of many people.

Many reports concerning the January 9 and 13 sightings in central Connecticut eventually found their way to us. Credible people felt they had seen something that cannot be explained in conventional terms, especially "ultralights in formation" and "power surges." If those theories do not explain the sightings and electrical abnormalities, we must look elsewhere for answers.

CHAPTER TWO ...

OF EPIDEMIC PROPORTIONS

When one looks at a single UFO sighting or experience, it is very difficult to make any sense of the true nature of the phenomenon. A single case study shows only a tiny portion of the entire picture, without revealing the staggering implications of a widespread epidemic. No matter how skeptical the reader may be, three things cannot be denied: UFO sightings exist, they persist, and they are part of a global phenomenon.

UFO investigators do not study UFOs; they study UFO reports. The modern era of UFO reports began in 1947, when a private pilot reported that he saw a number of unknown objects flying near the tops of the Cascade mountains. When he described the sighting, a reporter asked him what the objects looked like. He replied, "They looked like saucers skipping across water." Thus the term "Flying Saucer" was born. The pilot did not say the objects looked like saucers, but that they moved like a saucer skipping across the water. The objects that he saw were, in fact, boomerang in shape. In the years that followed, people started reporting objects that were saucer-shaped. Were witnesses assuming that the unknown objects were saucer-shaped and reporting them as such simply because they were called "Flying Saucers?" This is one of the many mysteries of Ufology (the study of UFOs).

Since the 1970s, reports of disk-shaped UFOs have been replaced by sightings of triangle- and boomerang-shaped objects. Some researchers feel that the difference in shape represents technological advances of this alien society. Others feel that the triangular design represents a new alien culture visiting earth. Whatever the answer, it is clear that these UFOs are much more aggressive than the disks reported in the 1950s and 1960s. They are not afraid to appear before thousands of people, or violate the restricted air space above military bases and nuclear reactors.

Below, we present a collection of some of the most well-documented sightings of triangular-boomerang UFOs. The Hudson Valley UFO sightings, described in chapter 1, were the first reports to get worldwide attention, and it is with those case studies that we will compare the other reports. We feel that these reports represent a large piece in the puzzle of understanding this complex phenomenon. We would like to thank our fellow researcher Bob Pratt, the Center for UFO Studies, and Dr. Willy Smith for helping complete this information.

The Triangle UFOs

1975–1989

October 27, 1975. Two young men, ages 18 and 22, were driving on a country road near Poland, Maine, at about 3:00 A.M. and saw what they thought were two huge truck lights in a field. As they got closer they realized that the lights belonged to one enormous object. As they watched, it rose into the air. The object was easily as large as a football field and triangular in shape. It moved down the road ahead of them. Then, from the distance of a half-mile, a blinding light hit them and they passed out. When they regained consciousness the UFO was above them, hovering. Frightened, they drove toward the town of Oxford, Maine and lost sight of the UFO. They drove for about a mile, until the car turned onto a side road of its own accord and stopped at a point overlooking a lake. They could then see the UFO again, above them. As they sat there they saw two small objects come up off the lake, descend in a falling-leaf pattern, then rise again, as if they were climbing steps. Suddenly, all three objects vanished.

Both men were quite ill for the following three days. They reported having strange experiences, such as seeing small cubes floating in the air. Both became paranoid and believed that the UFO was following them at all times. The older of the two said that a man in a black suit came to his trailer home and warned him not to speak of his experiences. The younger man soon moved to Oklahoma, but the other stayed in Maine and was finally persuaded to undergo hypnosis. During six sessions conducted by a physician, the man told of finding himself aboard the UFO, looking out a window, and seeing his friend still sitting in the car below. He was then led by a short, grayish creature into another part of the UFO, where he saw four more creatures and was given some sort of medical exam. He was then led back to the original room. The next thing he remembered was awakening in the car at the same time as his friend. The younger man was never reached for an interview.

January 24, 1978. In England, near Leicester and Hinckley, at least seventeen people reported seeing a delta-shaped object between 7:00 and 8:00 P.M. As in the Hudson Valley sightings, the object flew low overhead and made no noise. It was lit by steady red, blue, and yellow lights as it headed south from Leicester toward Hinckley, where it was seen by twelve more residents.

February 9, 1978. At 7:45 P.M., a huge triangular object was reported near South Lyon, Michigan in a town called Island Lake. Several residents saw it hovering near their homes. One resident, a former Air Force aircraft mechanic, reported seeing a boomerang-shaped object the size of three 747s with a "great intensity of light coming from the center fuselage area." It was heading west, flying at a slow speed. At least three adults and a number of children also saw the object, which made a slight humming noise. The slight noise confounded the ex-mechanic, who said a craft that size would have made enough noise to "blow out every window in the area." Police received close to two dozen calls about that sighting.

September 14–16, 1978. A series of sightings occurred throughout the country of Italy. Reports described numerous cigar-, disc-, and triangular-shaped objects. In the Alps near

Bolzano, rail workers saw a triangular object with two powerful lights. The object disappeared after a few moments, moving at great speed. At 5:50 A.M. on September 14th, people in Rome observed a triangular object for five minutes. At the same time, people near Florence reported seeing a cigar-shaped object. Early on the morning of the 16th, highway police near Rome received calls about a "luminous triangle" and "a beam of greenish light."

December 23, 1978. At 9:30 P.M., a newspaper sports reporter driving to Punta del Este, Uruguay on assignment saw a giant "V" formation of lights 300 to 400 meters away, along the slope of the Pan de Azucar (Sugar Loaf Hill). The lights were stationary, and he stopped to get a better look. It was an imposing sight, but since there was nothing he could do, he decided to continue his trip. Just a few moments later he saw a pair of bright lights in his rear view mirror. Thinking it was a truck, he pulled over to let it pass, but nothing happened. He again stopped and got out. The lights had disappeared; there was no truck. Somewhat alarmed, he got in his car again and began to drive, only to see a bright white light cross the road 500 meters ahead of him and perhaps 300 meters high, heading out to sea.

February 11, 1980. Between 10:00 P.M. and midnight, in western Argentina and Chile, hundreds of people in more than a dozen communities reported seeing a large, triangular object. The majority of the sightings occurred between 10:50 and 11:10 over a large area. Shortly before 11:00, the mayor and thirty-one other people in Ahilinco, a small community in the Neuquen Province 635 miles southwest of Buenos Aires, saw an object in the shape of a triangle high in the sky over the Andes Mountains. After remaining motionless for three minutes, the triangle disappeared, leaving only lights visible. After several more minutes, the lights began to gyrate and then blinked out, leaving a dark triangular-shaped object that was visible to the witnesses. The UFO then moved without a sound to the west, where it was soon out of sight. A similar object was also seen a short time later by residents in the nearby larger town of Chos Malal.

In the town of Ing Luis Huergo in the Rio Negro Province, a 22-year-old man returning home about 10:00 P.M. saw a bright light 200 meters away and about thirty meters in the air. The next thing he knew it was 11:00 P.M., an hour later, and he was in his car 18 kilometers away, near the town of Cervantes. The light was still visible just above the front of his car, which wouldn't start. He walked into town, but when he returned with a policeman the object was gone. He described it as "two big 'L's. Where the two 'legs' of the L joined was a kind of star. Inside the L was a square, and within the square a smaller one, which looked like a kind of TV screen." A mailman who lives two kilometers southeast of Cervantes said that at 10:55 P.M., he and four or five neighbors saw a large ball of light that projected a beam of light down to the ground. After three or four minutes it flew off to the north at great speed.

Between 10:45 and 11:00 P.M., numerous people in Chepes, Barrealito, Tamberies, and Chamical in San Juan Province, 600 miles to the north-northwest, saw a large triangular object with a "blue luminosity and a reddish hue" moving at great speed. Around 11:00 P.M., in Santiago, Chile, many people, including military and police personnel, saw an immense ball of light that projected two beams of light into the sky and down toward the ground. After ten minutes, the object began to wobble, then disappeared at "an incredible speed." Around 11:30 P.M., near El Medano in Cantamarca Province, Argentina, 400 miles north of Santiago, a doctor, his wife, and their three children saw an enormous ball of intense orange light that cast three beams of light; one to the left, one to the right, and one down on the ground. They observed it with five other people. After several minutes, the object shot off across the horizon at great speed.

At 11:45 P.M., in San Vicente in neighboring Santiago del Estero Province, about 100 miles northeast of El Mendano, witnesses saw a triangular object that shined intermittent green, red, and yellow lights toward the ground. The object remained motionless for five minutes, then disappeared quickly. Shortly before midnight, an unidentified object passed over the Pacific coast towns of Penco and Lirquen in Chile, just north of Concepcion and nearly 300 miles south of Santiago, then landed in the waters of the bay. It floated for about ten minutes, shining searchlights that lit the whole bay, then suddenly ascended and disappeared over the mountains to the east, leaving behind a trail of smoke that hung in the air for about two hours.

October 23, 1980. A huge triangular or boomerang-shaped object made repeated visits to the two adjoining copper-mining towns of Clifton and Morenci, Arizona, during October, November, and December. The most spectacular sightings occurred on October 23rd. On that night the object hovered above a football field where a high school band was practicing. All 110 members of the band, as well as thirty to forty parents sitting in the stands, saw the object, which appeared to be as big as the field itself and stayed throughout the entire rehearsal before drifting off. It was described as a "string of lights in a triangular shape." It would move and stop, move and stop, until it finally disappeared about the time the practice ended. Shortly before it was seen over the high school, five maintenance workers saw the UFO above a large copper smelting plant one mile west of the school, beyond a mountain ridge. They said it had twelve red lights on it and a big searchlight in the front.

The smelter has two smokestacks, 600 feet tall, 23 feet in diameter, and 130 feet apart. The object hovered directly over one of the smokestacks and appeared to shine a searchlight down into it. It then moved away, and shot off to the south, but suddenly stopped and returned. It passed over the smelter again, then moved out of sight over a huge open mine pit nearby. An investigator for the Aerial Phenomena Research Organization talked to five miners, who said they saw the object five miles west of Morenci about two hours later.

A number of people in Clifton and Morenci said that they had seen a diamond shaped object during the last three months of the year. One resident, a restaurant owner who claimed to have witnessed several sightings, said that he and another man saw a V-shaped object in April, 1980. The object had three or four lights on each side. It passed low overhead and suddenly split into two sections, with half the lights going one way and half the other way. Another witness, a woman, saw the triangular object as it passed over her. She said that the bottom looked "like little hardwood planks three or four inches wide, like a hardwood floor." The UFO hovered for several more seconds, then shot away at fantastic speed.

December 29, 1980. Two middle-aged women and the grandson of one were driving on a deserted country highway between the towns of New Caney and Dayton, Texas, around 9:00 P.M. They were on their way home to Dayton when they spotted a glowing red object on the horizon ahead of them. Several minutes later, it suddenly swooped down and hovered over the road a short distance ahead of them. It was a dazzlingly bright, enormous diamond-shaped object standing on one end. The glow was so bright they could barely stand to look at it. They stopped the car so that they could watch it. The object periodically belched flames from the bottom toward the road in a very unnerving manner. It would then would rise up a short distance, only to settle back down. All three people got out of the car, but the grandson was so terrified that the grandmother quickly got him and herself back inside. The driver walked to the front of the car and stood there for a short while. Her companion pleaded with her to get back into the car and she finally did. After about fifteen minutes, the object—which all this time had been making a loud noise accompanied by a constant beeping sound—finally rose up above the pine trees, turned over on its side, and slowly drifted south toward the nearby Gulf of Mexico. As it flew away it was surrounded by more than twenty military helicopters. The women later identified most of them from pictures as CH-47 Chinooks. The women and the boy drove home, all feeling ill. They suffered from nausea, severe headaches, diarrhea, reddening of the skin, stomach pains, extreme thirst, and loss of appetite. The driver, who was exposed to the object longer than the other two, was hospitalized several days later, her face blistered and badly swollen. She spent a month in the hospital, recovering. All three broke out in blisters and have since remained highly sensitive to heat. The two women lost most of their hair, which did grow back within six months. In the years that followed, all three suffered from unknown illnesses that many feel were caused by the close encounter with the UFO.

UFO investigators found others who had seen the glow of light from a distance that night, and other witnesses who had seen a large group of CH-47s in the area later that evening. They appeared to be searching for something as they moved fairly low across the sky. However, all government and military agencies denied having any aircraft in the area that night or knowing anything about the incident. All activity involving the object and helicopters occurred at fairly low altitude and would not have been picked up by radar at Houston International Airport, thirty miles to the south.

April 15, 1981. A man driving in the area of Mount Sunapee in New Hampshire at 7:35 P.M. saw a huge, triangular object with red lights. It first appeared as "two huge, bright stars" to the east and was stationary. Then "one of the stars seemed to fall several miles straight down" and began moving westward. As it approached, the object took on the appearance of a huge metal triangle with several red lights on the side and a very bright, high-intensity white light on the leading edge. The object looked very similar to "five B-52s in a low-altitude flight, flying in a staggered 'V' formation." The object flew "very low, lower than the hills," and passed right over the witness' car, moving toward the west.

October 31, 1981. Somewhere on the El Cajon mountain, forty kilometers west of Mendoza, Argentina, in the Andes, seven veteran mountain climbers camped for the night. The climbers were surprised by a bright light that rose rapidly and soundlessly, leaving a glow which reflected on the mountain. "It was as if someone had projected a light from a powerful reflector, and in that light one could see a kind of cloud which danced, as though you were looking at exhaust from automobiles reflecting in your headlights," said one climber. Another said, "The thing changed quickly into a brilliant sphere, and then you could see in the middle of it a kind of darkened hat-like shape...." Later, he said, the object disappeared and transformed itself into "white contrails which in a matter of seconds took on a triangular shape, and through the clouds a solid ship could be seen."

Mid-February, 1982. At approximately 9:00 P.M., near Bakersfield, Vermont, a woman driving home on Vermont Rt. 36 from St. Albans saw a large white light moving slowly through the sky about a mile and a half from Bakersfield. "It was quite low in the sky. At first I thought it was a plane about to land, so I flashed my headlights to warn it off the road. Then it started coming toward me." As the object got closer she could see it was triangular in shape. Before losing sight of it, she convinced herself it was a hang-glider or a hot air balloon. She turned into her driveway and was startled to see the glowing triangle in her own backyard. "It was just hovering there, about 25 feet from me," she said. She got out of her car, picked up her two bags of groceries, and started toward the house. "Then I stopped for a moment to look at the thing and I began to feel very frightened. It was obviously watching me." She called out for an upstairs neighbor but no one responded. Feeling fairly panicky, she began running toward her house, and she dropped her groceries on the way. "I looked down at the bags, then up at the sky. The thing was then moving right over my head, making absolutely no sound. Now I could see that it wasn't just one light, it had many lights all across the bottom. It was much bigger than I'd thought, maybe as big as a football field." The object moved away without a sound. She ran inside and woke up her neighbor, who stayed with her the rest of the night. Neither woman would go outside and get the groceries. The next morning the object was nowhere to be seen and the groceries were frozen in the snow.

January 18, 1983. At least 200 people witnessed two triangular objects with flashing lights that moved slowly through the skies above Cardiff, Wales. Among the witnesses were twenty-two pupils at an elementary school and two detectives working in another part of the city. "There was a large main cluster of lights at the front, shaped a bit like a Zeppelin, followed by a triangular group of lights," said one detective. Another witness was a 40-year-old aircraft engineer who had worked for the RAF for fifteen years. He saw the object while coaching a boys' soccer team, and was certain it could not have been an aircraft. "We stopped playing to watch it," he said. "I couldn't fathom why the lights were so far apart. It was close, perhaps 600 to 1,000 feet up. It must have been 300 feet across, so it could not have been an aircraft. The thing I really don't understand is that it made no noise."

January 6, 1986. Somewhere around 7:45 P.M., a 53-year-old woman and her husband, a construction worker, were returning home to Hampstead after dining in Wilmington,

North Carolina, when they saw lights about 400 feet above U.S. 17. It was a boomerang-shaped object as big as two football fields. "It just came over real slow; he estimated about fifteen to twenty miles per hour," said the wife. "I believe it was the most terrifying feeling I've ever had in my life...I caught myself trying to hide from the lights behind my husband. I begged him to get back in the car...but it was like he was mesmerized...It scared me so bad, I cried. It left me with a very uneasy feeling, a very humble feeling. I did not want to see anything like that again. But three or four days later, I would have given anything to see it again."

April 20, 1986. Sometime during the night, in the mountainous areas of Kremmling, Dillon, and Silverthorne, Colorado, local officials in two counties received calls about stationary lights in the sky. One Kremmling police officer saw the lights and then was informed of sightings over the Green Mountain Reservoir near the Grand-Summit county line. He hurried to get there and found a large group of officers from both counties watching the lights. Through a high-powered telescope, the object looked to be triangular in shape, with lights on the outer edges. The object hovered for a while, then took off to the southwest. The most starling aspect of the occurrence was the evasive action taken by a jet plane, which all present saw veer around the object. The Kremmling police officer said the group watched the lights for about two hours.

November 24, 1986. At 11:00 P.M., in Waukesha, Wisconsin, a 29-year-old-man driving home saw flashing red lights in the sky to the southeast. He thought at first that they were the lights on a radio station tower but, as he got closer, he could see that the lights were spinning around like police car lights. "But it was up in the sky, no more than 200 feet high and it was hovering in the air and rotating," he said. He stopped in a parking lot about 150 yards away from the object, got out, and watched in utter amazement. The object was shaped like a flattened triangle and was perhaps seventy-five feet wide. At each corner were pairs of flashing red lights. On the sides were pairs of white and red lights that did not flash. The craft seemed to be dark brown or black in color. As it hovered, it rotated slowly and made no sound. After two or three minutes, the witness decided to get a closer look, but as he drove closer, the object stopped rotating and began moving away, staying in front of him and very low. It then headed over a grove of trees and was lost to sight.

March 9, 1987. From 8:30 to 11:00 P.M. at Devils Lake, North Dakota, a number of residents, including two off-duty police officers, saw a diamond-shaped, multi-colored object that hovered and moved quickly over the area. The two officers watched the object for fifteen to twenty minutes. It had red, yellow, and green lights that appeared to blink or possibly rotate. The object hovered at an altitude of about 500 feet, but left in a "quick manner that was considerably faster than any plane."

April 17, 1987. At 10:20 P.M. in the town Hutchinson, Kansas, a couple sitting on their porch saw a triangular object "gliding by," going east. It had no lights and made no noise. "We couldn't see it until the street lights reflected on it," said the wife. "It was like a boomerang with the apex pointed forward. It was hard to tell how big it was. It wasn't as big as an airplane." The color was "gun-metal blue," according to the husband, who was certain it wasn't a plane.

October, 1987. In Worthing, England, two men reported seeing a glowing object in the sky around 9:00 P.M.. One, a car salesman, said, "It was hovering, looking at first like a shaft of light, right in the middle of the sky. It seemed to change shape, from a rugby ball, to a hemisphere, to a triangle, then to a square. Then it gradually shrank into a red dot and disappeared...It was about the size of a full moon seen quite low." The other man said, "It was amorphous. It kept changing shape. I have never experienced anything like it before and we saw it clearly for twenty to twenty-five minutes." Two days later an eighteen-year-old insurance clerk spotted a strange yellow light over the same area. "It sort of stretched as if it was trying to break apart. It was as though some invisible hand was playing with plasticine."

October 26, 1988. In the Porterville, California area, hundreds of people reported seeing objects in the sky sometime during the night. Among the witnesses were a couple and their son, who were sitting in the back of their pickup truck at a drive-in movie. "We could see individual lights," the wife said. "Each ship was V-shaped, with one light a little ahead of the other. Red and white lights were located along the outer edges of the Vs, with a large red light at the back of each object." Another witness said, "There were a series of red lights behind the main object. I would say three lights. When it flew in front of the moon, there weren't any wings." Other witnesses speculated that the craft could be stealth bombers, but officials at nearby Northrop Corporation denied that any of their craft were flying that night. The only other airstrip in the area is Castle Air Force Base, and only B-52s fly out of there.

December 28, 1988. Many people near the towns of Lajas and Cabo Rojo, Puerto Rico, reported that they had seen jet fighters chase a small UFO over the Sierra Bermeja, a small mountain ridge, early in the day. At 7:45 that evening, they saw a large, triangular UFO that seemed to have some kind of extended appendage on its frontal section, with many brilliantly colored lights constantly blinking on and off. It was slightly curved at its rear end and had a gray, metallic structure. A large, central yellow light was emitted from a big, bulging, luminous, circular, concave appendage. The triangle had brilliant yellow lights on its right "wing tip" and red lights on its left. As the people watched, two jet fighters tried to intercept it. They passed in front of it, at which time the UFO veered to the left and made a turn back, reducing its speed. The jets tried to intercept it three times, and then the UFO decreased its speed, almost stopping in mid-air.

One jet stationed itself at the right side of the UFO, the other at its rear. Suddenly, the jet in back just disappeared on top of or inside the UFO. One witness was watching with binoculars and never saw the jet emerge from beyond the UFO. The second jet remained very close to the right side of the object, looking very small in comparison. As the UFO flew a little to the west, the second jet also disappeared, apparently inside the UFO, and its engine noise stopped. After trapping the jets, the object lowered its position and came very close to the ground over a small pond known as Saman Lake. It remained stationary in mid-air for a moment, then straightened its corners and emitted a big flash of yellow light from the central ball of light. It then divided itself in the middle into two different and distinct triangular sections. The triangle to the right was illuminated in yellow and the other in red. They both shot off at great speed, one to the southeast, the other to the northwest. Red sparks could be seen falling when the object divided itself. A retired Army veteran living in the area said that at 8:20 P.M., a group of black helicopters arrived and flew over the Sierra Bermeja and Laguna Cartagena areas, without lights until midnight. They appeared to be searching for something. UFO researchers checked with all Puerto Rican and U.S. Government agencies that might have knowledge of the incident, but all denied knowing anything about what happened. The investigator, Jorge Martin, of Rio Piedras, Puerto Rico, said that a week later a U.S. Naval officer whom he could not identify confirmed all that happened. He said that radar tapes had been sent to Washington D.C. and that a lid of secrecy had been placed on the whole affair. Shortly after the incident, the local government "leased" the area of the Sierra Bermeja and Laguna Cartagena to the federal government, reportedly because the government is building a Voice of America radio station there. The Voice of America is an international short-wave radio broadcasting system that is operated secretly by the CIA and used for propaganda.

January 30, 1989. Before dawn, a 30-foot fishing boat had just rounded Shagwong Point after leaving Montauk Harbor, Long Island, New York, en route to cod fishing grounds. For about ten minutes the captain watched a strange light on the water just north of the Montauk Lighthouse. The light seemed to come from an unknown object in the sky. The captain changed course slightly and began to head toward the light. He thought at first that it was a helicopter, but when he got close to the light he was surprised to hear no sound. He also noticed that his onboard radar system quit working, as did a number of other electrical devices. Apprehensive, the captain turned off the running lights and the engine. To him and two crewman, the light appeared to be square-shaped. It was less than a mile away. Then the light began moving toward the boat, bobbing around and moving from side to side as it came closer. "I really thought it was going to stop right over us," the captain said. He also noticed then that, seen at closer range, the object was triangular or diamond-shaped and appeared to be about 150 feet long. The only noise was a slight humming sound. "It turned belly up and cruised west, then south, climbing higher and higher until it disappeared," the captain said. As soon as the UFO vanished the radar started working once again.

May 4, 1989. An Easton, Connecticut resident reported seeing an object shaped like a flying wing between 9:30 and 10:00 P.M. The object had red, yellow, and blue lights in the back and a blinking red light on the right side. It flew over the tree line behind his house. A woman in Trumbull, eight miles to the east, reported seeing a low-flying, V-shaped object as big as a football field that made a faint humming sound. The object had many colored lights and looked like a Christmas tree in the sky. At about 10:00 P.M., an engineer driving to his home in Trumbull saw a cluster of three concentrated, bright red and white lights. He decided it was a helicopter, but thought it was peculiar. It was traveling slowly toward Bridgeport, just to the south. The engineer stopped, and the red and white lights disappeared. The object looked like a blue boomerang, "like a giant hang glider with soft blue lights." Intrigued, he went home and got his father, who had worked for the Sikorsky helicopter company for fifteen years and could identify a helicopter by its sound. The two followed the object to a former golf course, where it disappeared. The father was unable to identify the craft. "I can't find a feasible answer," the engineer said. "It would have taken a tremendous amount of money and energy to do this. I did some triangulation, and it was between 800 and 1,300 feet above my head. The lights changed color and a blue 'V' formed out of nowhere. I don't know how someone could pull this off, or why they would want to." Police in both Easton and Trumbull received several phone calls of UFO sightings.

October 9, 1989. In Winnipeg, Manitoba, Canada, between 11:15 PM and 2:15 A.M., an amateur astronomer waiting for an anticipated meteor shower sighted nine unidentified objects. Between 11:20 to 11:30 P.M., a large, boomerang-shaped object flew north to south over the city. At 11:35 P.M., three ball-shaped objects flew along the same path, followed by another boomerang-shaped object going east to west. At 12:07 A.M., three more ball-shaped objects flew over the city in a straight line, with a fourth trailing slightly to the west. At 1:08 A.M., another boomerang flew north to south, but this time lower in the sky. In his report to the Manitoba Planetarium, the witness said he was sure these weren't planes or satellites. "I used to help build planes and I've seen lots of satellites," he said. "These things had no lights. They were strictly self-illuminated objects. They were very clear and very sharp." Ed Barker, the planetarium producer and director of the Manitoba Centre for UFO Studies, said the planetarium had received a number of calls at the end of the summer regarding boomerang-shaped objects in the sky.

The Belgium Triangular UFO Sightings

1989–1993

One of the most dramatic series of sightings of triangular UFOs comes from Belgium, one of the smallest and most densely populated countries in Europe. Since October of 1989, thousands of people in this tiny country of ten million have seen a huge, triangular UFO, reported to be very similar to the Hudson Valley UFO. The sightings and descriptions of the object were so similar to those made in New England in the early 1980s that UFO researchers called it "The European Hudson Valley UFO Case." Since early 1990, we have been in contact with Belgian UFO investigator Patrick Ferryn. Mr. Ferryn is co-founder of an organization called SOBEPS (The Belgium Society for the Study of Special Phenomena). His organization has gathered reports from over 1200 witnesses regarding 700 different sightings. It is estimated that as many as 10,000 people have seen this UFO, which is reported to be larger than an aircraft carrier.

When we first started receiving data on the Belgian sightings, the material presented a problem; all of the reports and data were in French. It took quite an effort to translate the material, but what the data revealed was very interesting, to say the least. In many ways the sightings did parallel those reported in the Hudson Valley and Connecticut. In a letter Mr. Ferryn wrote to our fellow researcher, Bob Pratt, he said, "It was really astonishing for us to read the preface of *Night Siege*. Changing only a few words, the same thing could be written to give an account of what is going on here."

Since Belgium is a small country and the sightings were so numerous, the researchers of SOBEPS had unusual cooperation from their government. We in the United States should be so lucky; instead, our government has gone out of its way to explain away and discredit not only sightings of UFOs, but the people who report and investigate them. The Ministry of the Interior ordered Belgian police and military personnel to cooperate fully with the SOBEPS researchers, to turn over copies of all sightings to them, and to contact them when new sightings took place. In addition, the Ministry of Defense ordered the Belgian Air Force to authorize the researchers to contact radar operators, pilots, and military personnel who had sightings. The Belgian Air Force also arranged two military aircraft and their crews to be at the disposal of SOBEPS for UFO research.

The sightings seem to have started in October of 1989 near Eupen, close to the Dutch border, then progressed to the city of Brussels, and finally to the French border. The area involved is 120 miles long. Most of the sightings were at night, very few during the day. The majority of the sightings were Close Encounters of the First Kind: sighting a UFO within 200 yards. Among the witnesses were more than 200 members of the Belgian military, as well as police officers, pilots, air traffic controllers, scientists, and many other people from professional fields.

Most of the witnesses reported seeing a dark triangular or boomerang-shaped object that had several bright lights in the front and a red light located in the middle or at the end. Often people reported flashing lights along the 'V' of the triangle or boomerang. These reports almost exactly match descriptions of the Hudson Valley UFO, in which witnesses reported a very dark mass behind lights that sometimes were seen to flash.

Plate 2. Photograph and computer enhancement of the UFO that was seen in Belgium from 1988 through 1992. This triangular UFO is very similar to objects reported in the United States.

Some of the reported UFOs in Belgium were smaller triangular objects. These smaller versions of the bigger ship seemed to be present at most of the close encounter cases. In the Hudson Valley we also documented sightings of a large object and at least two smaller ones. As in the Belgium "flap" (an outbreak of UFO sightings in a specific geographic area), the smaller object or objects were present during many close encounters cases in Putnam and Dutchess county, New York. In both countries this smaller object seemed to be about 50 feet in size. In both the Hudson Valley sightings and the Belgian flap, the UFO moved very slowly, much too slowly for any conventional aircraft. At other times it would accelerate to fantastic speeds and appear far on the horizon, then sometimes flash back directly above the witnesses. The object was almost always noiseless, but sometimes a faint electric hum was audible.

The Belgium object would make slow, 180-degree turns while hovering. This was also reported in the Hudson Valley, where witnesses stated that the UFO would turn as if on a wheel as it hovered. In the close encounter cases, the witnesses in Belgium reported that they saw structure underneath the object, with heavy metal parts, criss-cross effects, and some type of tubular network. In the close encounter cases that we have investigated in the Hudson Valley, the same kind of structure was reported on over twenty occasions. Some people in Belgium reported that the object's shape appeared to change, and that red globes of lights were seen emerging from an opening in the bottom of the UFO. In the Hudson Valley case, a red globe of light was often seen entering or leaving the object from the underside. We also heard many reports from people who encountered this red globe of light. In some cases it circled their car while they were driving. On other occasions, it entered homes of UFO witnesses by passing right through a window without breaking the glass.

The Belgium UFO was seen over populated areas. According to SOBEPS researcher Ferryn, who visited the Hudson Valley several years ago, the landscapes of Belgium and the Hudson Valley are very similar. Some Belgian witnesses said that they signaled the UFO with their car lights and the UFO flashed its lights back. Similar reports are also present in the Hudson Valley case.

On November 29, 1989 the Belgium UFO was seen by hundreds of people around Eupen. On that night SOBEPS collected 120 reports. One sighting was made by two police officers. While in their patrol car, they were lit up by a beam of light coming from a dark triangle equipped with three projecting structures and a red, winking light. The object was huge and made a faint humming sound as it hovered at an altitude of 600 to 900 feet. One officer said that the light was so bright that he could read by it. The object then moved to the direction of nearby La Gileppe Dam, where it hovered for forty-five minutes. It then moved about thirteen miles southwest and hovered over the city of Spa for approximately thirty minutes before disappearing.

Perhaps one of the most important sighting dates was on March 30, when the UFO was witnessed by army and police officers around Wavre, about fifteen miles southeast of Brussels. In addition to these visual sightings, at least two radar installations around Brussels also tracked the UFO. All military and civilian planes in Belgian airspace have a device installed in them called a transponder. This device emits a coded signal that permits immediate identification of the aircraft. The UFO was tracked on radar moving very slowly, about thirty miles an hour, much too slowly for any aircraft. It also changed altitude and direction frequently. The object did not send any transponder code, so orders were given for two F-16 fighter jets to intercept and identify the unknown aircraft.

As the fighters approached the location of the object they both spotted the UFO on their radar screens. They were able to lock on to the object with visual cameras and when they did, the UFO appeared triangular on their screens. At the same time, the encounter was being recorded with onboard video cameras. The pilots began the procedure to lock on to the UFO with their missiles guidance systems. Although they had no intention of firing, the system could be used to help identify the intruder. This required the pilot to lock on to the object by radar for at least five seconds, but they did not even have time to do this. Before a missile lock could be achieved, the UFO increased in speed from 280 to close to 2,000 miles an hour, at the same time descending from 10,000 to 6,000 feet in one second. This fantastic maneuver would have created a force of over 35Gs, enough to kill any human aboard a conventional aircraft. The limit a human pilot can endure in a supersonic jet is just under 8Gs.

After the UFO reached 6,000 feet, it then dove rapidly toward the ground, to an altitude of less than 600 feet. In doing so it disappeared from the radar of the fighters and the ground stations. The pilots then lost visual sight of the object.

Members of SOBEPS were allowed to see the reports, listen to the tape recordings of the pilots, and view the taped footage made by the pilots of the F-16s. This was the first time that a government agency cooperated fully with the media and civilian researchers in a UFO case.

One explanation proposed was that the Belgian UFO was the American-built F-117 Stealth Fighter. The rumors were partially confirmed by a French newspaper that interviewed Air Force Colonel Tom Tolin. Col. Tolin was quoted as saying that "F-117s are flown in Europe during night missions, sometimes by pilots of the United Kingdom's Royal Air Force, but we are not authorized to tell you when or where they are flying." It seems to me that the way the object maneuvered would rule out conventional aircraft of any kind. Later, in 1989 to 1991, some skeptics used the Stealth theory to also explain the sightings in the Hudson Valley.

Our personal opinion is that the Belgium and Hudson Valley UFOs are the same class of object, and that there is no evidence to indicate any man-made, conventional explanation for the sightings.

Mountain City, Tennessee

1994–1995

What started as an average evening at home with his family, turned into the starting point of an adventure for Steve Smith—an adventure in which he may not have wanted to partake. On the evening of November 15, 1994, at 7:10 P.M., he was at home playing a computer game. Hearing a helicopter outside—the fifth one that day—he went out to investigate. At first, all Steve could see was a flashing blue strobe light. As he got ready to go back into his house, he was amazed to see a huge craft fly over the hill. It had eleven lights glowing on the bottom and two small lights on the front. Steve described the movement of the object as drifting rather than actively flying. He ran into the house to tell his family, and they all went out the front door to get a better look at it. They were able to watch it for about fifteen minutes. It looked saucer-shaped, but they could not make out a geometric outline. The only sound that came from the object was that of air rushing over it as it moved. After this first incredible sighting, both Steve's son and wife were rushed to the emergency room at 4:00 A.M. due to high fevers. The cause of the fevers was never known, but our files contain a number of cases in which people became ill after a UFO passed close to them. Why Steve did not become ill is not known for sure, but UFOs seem to emit radiation that affects the human immune system. Perhaps his son and wife already had a virus in their system, and it incubated at a greater speed because the UFO did in fact lower their immunity to infection.

Over the course of the following week Steve wanted to report his sighting to someone who might give him an explanation for what he had seen. The local and state police were of no help whatsoever. However, to Steve's surprise, a call to the 1-800 directory provided a promising phone number. On December 15, at 3:00 P.M. he called the number for what was supposed to be Patrick Air Force Base in Florida. He got a duty officer who transferred him to a colonel, who said that he was a social psychologist. He started asking Steve questions about his encounter, as if he was reading them from a "UFO Questionnaire Form." He wanted to fly Steve down to Florida to make a statement. Steve had to decline; he was unable to travel at that time because of job demands. Steve asked the colonel if he knew what the object was that he had seen. The colonel said, "We know that they are unidentified, but we don't know if they are extra-terrestrial or if they are from here." He quickly transferred Steve to a major, who said that he was an audiologist. Steve could barely hear the major because there was a communications radio in the background that was very loud. The radio seemed to be transmitting communications from two fighter pilots. Steve could clearly hear them say, "Eagle has UFO on screen will disperse now…(1 min.)…struck! The Eagle has struck." The major talking on the phone yelled out, "Someone get that radio, I've got a (some kind of code name for Mr. Smith) on the telephone." Then Steve heard one of the pilots on the radio say, "It's on the ground...Professor, you've got to get down here now!" The major yelled out, "That cannot be disclosed!" He got back on the phone with Steve and said, "Sorry there is so much noise here. I've got to go." He took Steve's telephone number and said that either he would call back, or Steve should call him back. When Steve called the next day, using the same 800 number, he reached the helicopter rescue unit instead. This time a woman answered. She knew nothing about anyone Steve was trying to contact. The same number was tried by our research team a number of times, with the same results. The number was disconnected the next day, then put back in service a few weeks later. Further research has shown that any 800 numbers for the military are directed to either Andrews Air Force Base or the Pentagon.

Since then, the object and others like it have been sighted by an increasingly large number of people. They can be seen on almost any clear night. Mr. Smith, being quite tenacious, has done a lot of follow-up, asking people in the area if they have seen anything strange. A couple who own a small cafe on a hilltop spent the summer watching the objects sweep the area. Another man admitted to having seen these objects as far back as three years ago. So with all of this activity, why is it that the TriCity International Airport has no knowledge of any low flying military or civilian aircraft in the area that is covered by their radar?

More recently, the object has been seen flying lower, slower, and alone. On previous sightings it had been seen in the company of another object, smaller than the original. Occasionally, they were joined by a third object, completely different from the first two. The original object was finally seen crossing in front of the moon, allowing Mr. Smith to see a definite geometric shape. He described the first two objects as equilateral triangles, while the third seemed to be a circle and was much smaller than the first two.

A local TV station, WCYB in Bristol, Virginia, has been mentioning the UFO a great deal. One evening right before the weather news, the weatherman said that there had been a sighting, and anyone with a camera who could get it on video would have the pleasure of seeing their pictures on the air the next night. Steve went out to look for it. He was able to see it but did not own a camera. Someone else did, and the UFO was shown on TV the very next night!

Numerous unmarked black helicopters, reported to be flying at low altitude, are getting to be a regular sight in the area. Only a few departments in the government are allowed to fly without any markings. They include the CIA, NSA, and NSC (Central Intelligence Agency, the National Security Agency, and the National Security Council).

Mr. Smith wishes that he had never seen this inexplicable object, for now he is plagued with the desire to know what it is and what is it doing. As of the writing of this book, this series of sightings are still under investigation, and we are hoping for new information in the near future.

The English Flying Triangles

1995

For the past few years the English in the Derby area have been plagued with a series of sightings they have nicknamed the "Flying Triangles." On March 16, 1995, in the early morning hours, two brothers were driving along Route A52 near Willington, South Derbyshire. They were on their way to Swarkstone and had just gone around a tight bend in the road when they saw a very large, triangular object coming directly toward them. It had approximately nine large, three-dimensional light panels, like blocks of white light, underneath the aircraft. Because of the lights' intensity, it was very difficult to make out the outline while it was overhead, but it appeared to be a type of delta wing. The brothers stopped their car and got out to watch for several minutes; because of the cold they didn't stay outside very long. While watching the craft travel very slowly, they wondered why it didn't stall out and lose altitude. They were able to hear a sound like a jet engine, and figured it must be some kind of night surveillance craft.

On the very next night the object was seen by a couple in the Sinfin Moor, Derby area. It was their first encounter with the "Flying Triangle." The wife said, "You could see it very clearly. It was very low and slowly moving right over the rooftops. I couldn't believe it. I was flabbergasted. It was massive, bigger than a plane. We weren't frightened, just fascinated." The husband saw it again on April 4 at about one in the morning. On that occasion it was stationary for a long period of time, and moved more slowly than before. It made no sound and appeared to be gliding. Its lights were red and white.

On Wednesday, April 26, at 11:45 P.M., a language teacher was getting ready to go to bed and noticed an illuminated aircraft approaching her home. She lives on Stenson Road, Derby near the East Midlands Airport, so she was used to having low-flying aircraft over her house. This one was different. It was heading in from the wrong direction, and seemed black and huge. As it got closer she was able to make out the shape of a large, black, triangular craft. It had a white light in each corner and a red flashing light almost in the center. She was able to hear a faint engine noise, but nothing like the usual sound of a jet aircraft. She got a clear view of the underside; it was definitely a triangle, quite sharply defined, with no wings or tail.

Another sighting took place on April 28 in the vicinity of Spondon, Derby. A resident of the area was driving along Route A52 in the direction of Nottingham, about four miles outside of Derby. It was almost 8:00 P.M., but not quite dark. He noticed a slow moving light in the sky, but because of the turns in the road he was unable to give it any real attention. However, when he turned off the road at a junction he stopped and looked for the lights again, and found them. The lights appeared as an equilateral triangle, not too bright, but all equal in their brightness. The "Flying Triangle" was traveling point first, and a pulsating red light was visible off center in the middle. He was also able to make out a dim green light in the back, but this was only seen at a distance.

He watched the object for about thirty seconds. As it slowly passed on his (the driver's) side, he tried to roll down the window to get a better view. He thought he was able to make out a triangular silhouette against the sky, but he was unable to hear any sound. He used to live near the East Midlands Airport so he was familiar with low-flying aircraft. This object's lights were much too dim to be landing lights, and they were not on the wingtips as they would be on a plane.

He thought the object might have been a helicopter, except that the back two lights were too far apart, and helicopters make a great deal of noise.

On May 1, one of the members of the Southern Paranormal Investigations Group, based in Hampshire, had a surprise sighting. Darren Collins was visiting friends on holiday in a place called King's Newton. As he began to leave for his home, friends told him that if he cut through a little lane that was up ahead, he would come out on Route 514, which was the way he needed to go. He had traveled almost to the junction of 514 when a number of lights in a field caught his attention. He thought, "I am not going to miss this!" So he pulled over and got out of the car, leaving it running, and walked about a hundred yards up the road.

The object was just floating in the air. It was absolutely still, and seemed to be triangular in shape. There were lights in each corner and a flashing red light in the center. Darren could not believe what he was seeing. There was no way it was a plane. Just prior to the sighting he had seen an airplane overhead. This object was something else. It was only about 600 yards away and 150 feet up in the air. He stood for about two minutes, caught up in the wonder of the experience. Then, for whatever reason, Darren decided to shout at it. He yelled, "Come here, come over here!" He doesn't know if it was just a coincidence, but the object moved slightly to the right, then "took off and greatly accelerated," disappearing from view within three seconds. "It was traveling flat—face first, not point first, and there was not a sound." The object moved off in the direction of Barrow-on-Trent, going northeast.

Also in May, a young photography student living in the Southdowns Farm, Cornwall area had a sighting of a similar object. She reported a large triangular object with three bright, white lights arranged in the same pattern described in previous sightings, and a pulsing, off-center red light. However, her sighting was a bit different from the rest; jet fighters brought her attention to the object. She was attracted by the noise of the fighters, and looked up to see them in a triangular formation around this object. The fighters were moving faster than the triangle and were out of sight in a minute, while the UFO was visible for another full minute! Once the fighters were out of sight she could hear no noise coming from the area of the object. It appeared to be floating rather than flying, and was moving at a slower speed than the jet fighters were able to maintain.

It is clear that some of the case studies presented in this chapter are contact cases. It is our belief that all close encounter cases are not accidental, but are in fact a method of communication between the person and the intelligence behind the UFO phenomenon. In many cases those people who have had a close encounter continue to have sightings and finally have an abduction experience.

CHAPTER THREE ...

ENCOUNTER ON INTERSTATE 84

We return to the north-eastern section of the United States, which has become a hotbed of all types of paranormal and UFO activity. In past years the state of Connecticut has been an area of few UFO reports, but this is no longer true. Since 1985, most of the state has seen a dramatic rise not only in the number of UFO sightings, but also in other, related experiences, especially cases of abduction and contact. As a result of this increase in paranormal activity, a great number of groups and clubs have formed to explore what is going on. We have been contacted by many of these clubs and asked to be advisors in some capacity, but declined. We feel that our research should be in the hands of experienced researchers, rather than individuals who look at the subject as a sort of hobby.

We would like to make it very clear that the world of the paranormal, which includes UFOs, contains very real phenomena. Most people who start investigating UFO reports look at it as sort of a hobby. No matter how open your mind, there is always an element of doubt as to whether or not such things really exist. However, once you experience a UFO sighting for yourself, the subject is no longer a hobby, game, or curiosity. The paranormal becomes a part of reality, and your view of everything changes. Phil has been investigating UFOs and the paranormal for over two decades. During this time, he has seen enough to convince him that these mysterious occurrences are very real. We both take the investigation of UFOs very seriously. When we receive reports of encounters with UFOs, or of other related activities, we take them seriously, but we still investigate using objectivity and the scientific method.

Below we present a well-documented series of UFO sightings that took place in south-central Connecticut between May 26 and 29, 1988. The UFO was witnessed by many people, who were sure that it was not of this world.

Was it an Ultralight?

On May 26 between 9:30 and 10:15 P.M., more than 200 people between the towns of Danbury and Waterbury, Connecticut, called local and state police to report a huge object with bright lights flying very low near Interstate Highway 84. People reported their sightings to the state police, who called police in Southbury and were told that the object was nothing more than a group of ultralight aircraft. These small planes supposedly departed from Candlewood airport, flying in a close formation with colored lanterns hanging from the bottoms of their planes. The police also said that the planes were painted all black, so all that could be seen from the ground were the lights.

Many of the witnesses who saw the UFO that night found this explanation very hard to accept. Mrs. Betty Proulx of Middlebury viewed the object with her husband. She said that the UFO hovered over her house without a sound for over two minutes and then projected a brilliant beam of white light to the ground to form a perfect, well-defined circle. There is no doubt in the mind of Mr. Proulx that he saw one solid object, not a number of objects in formation. When Mr. and Mrs. Proulx heard the explanation offered by the local authorities they could not accept it as a description of what they had seen. Mr. Proulx was in the air division of the Navy and was very familiar with all types of aircraft. He told us, "It was one craft, and like no aircraft that I have ever seen in my life."

Another witness to the UFO that night was Mr. Randy Etting, a commercial airline pilot with over thirty years of experience and thousands of hours in the air. Mr. Etting said that the idea that the UFO was a number of small aircraft in formation is "the prattling of idiots." Mr. Etting observed the lights from his home in Newtown at about 9:45 P.M. He said that there were at least eight lights of different colors in a boomerang or half circle pattern, flying very close together and without a sound. As the object passed near his home he observed it with binoculars. Mr. Etting could tell that the UFO was one solid object because when the lights turned, they all turned at once. He told us that, observed through binoculars, it appeared that there was a distortion around the lights, as if heat or energy was coming from the dark area of the UFO. He watched the object with his neighbors and his son for over ten minutes as it slowly drifted to the north-west. Mr. Etting finished his report by saying, "You'd think that in all the years I was flying, I would have seen something strange that I couldn't explain. Who would think that the first time I saw a UFO it would be from the ground. I can tell you that this was like no aircraft that I have ever seen in my life. This thing was huge, at least the size of several 747s. The thing that amazed me was how something so large could move so slowly, with no engine noise. An aircraft half that size would have to be using its engines at almost 90% to stay in the air and move that slow."

While the Etting party watched the UFO, it was passing close to I-84. More than a dozen cars pulled over to view the object as it passed overhead. We know that the Newtown police sent several cars to investigate, as did the Connecticut State Police. Although we were unable to obtain the reports of the state police, the local police let us read the officers' reports of the object that they saw. In the police reports it is clear that the Newtown officers who observed the object had no idea what it was. The police report called the object "a UFO of unknown origin," not a formation of planes with colored lights on them.

Mr. Charles Tuperman was on the highway that night and saw the object as it passed over his car. Below is a transcript of his sighting account, as told to us one week after his encounter with the giant UFO.

"It was about 9:30 or so and I was driving east on 84 around the Southbury area when I noticed these lights ahead of me. They were low; it looked like a 747 was going to land on the highway. This thing had about ten lights in a kind of half-circle, and the lights were yellow, green, blue, white, and red. This thing was going very slow, moving from the east to the west. All of a sudden everyone on both sides of the highway began slamming on their brakes and pulling over to the side of the road. It was a dangerous thing to do since there were several trucks apparently trying to do the same thing and they took much longer to stop. I saw one truck almost jackknife because the car in front of him stopped so fast he had to brake hard and swerve out of the way. I pulled over and watched this thing pass directly over the westbound lanes. I saw a dark mass behind the lights and there was no sound. I saw the lights of a state trooper just ahead of me and I figured he was called to see what was going on. Then, while I was watching the UFO, all the lights got ten times brighter for about fifteen seconds or so and then they slowly faded to the same brilliance as when I first saw them. When it did this it really scared me, because I thought that it might give off some kind of radiation that might affect me in some way. I wanted to get going because I thought there was some type of an invasion or something. I just wanted to go home to be with my wife and kids. It was as if I had to get home to protect them. Besides, I was also afraid of some trucker coming along and plowing into me. I watched the UFO as it turned slightly and went west and I soon lost it over the hills. I turned on my radio for news, but I didn't hear anything about any sightings of UFOs on any of the local stations."

The UFO was so bright and large that it was only a matter of time before someone would come forward with a photograph. To our surprise we were contacted by a person of high standing in the Southbury area who took a color photograph of the UFO as it hovered near I-84. The person is a state trooper, and to protect his identity we cannot use his name, but he has given us permission to use the photograph in this book. We will refer to this now ex-law enforcement officer as David. We think this is one of the best nighttime still photographs ever taken of a UFO.

The Photograph

David was on Interstate 84 on official business when he saw the lights in the sky. The lights were in the northwest at the time. There had already been a number of calls to headquarters about a large, unknown object in the sky. The concern at the time was that it might be an aircraft in some kind of trouble. David saw the object heading east. As he watched, the UFO got much brighter. All of its lights seemed to glow intensely, as if they were burning flares. He pulled off to the side of the road and got out his camera. The UFO was about forty-five degrees above the horizon at this time, and almost motionless. Due to the traffic, David had time to take only one picture. His camera was a 35mm with a 50mm lens at F/1.8. He used Kodacolor 400 film at an exposure of 1/60th of a second. The object then moved toward the east without a sound. During our interview, David told us that he was sure that it was one solid object. To him, it looked as if the lights were connected to a dark mass. In the original negative you could actually see a hint of this structure.

Several photo experts looked at the image of the UFO on film. They are sure that the object is not a hoax and that it is, in fact, a very large object in the sky. The photograph was examined by Dr. Willy Smith, a scientist of some repute, and Dr. Bruce Macabee, a military photo analyst. Both scientists agree that the object is very large. Estimates based on the

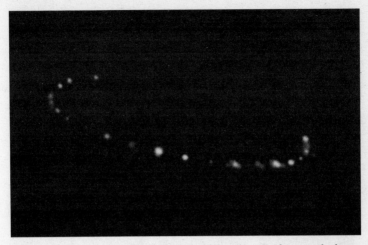

Plate 3. The Waterbury Elliptical UFO. This UFO was photographed near Waterbury, Connecticut on I-84 by a Connecticut law enforcement officer on May 26, 1988. The image has been analyzed by a number of experts. It has been determined that this is an enormous object less than a mile from the camera.

image on the film in relation to the distance of the photographer, and the type of lens used, show that the UFO is anywhere from 650 to 1600 feet across! Dr. Macabee stated that the lights on the object are unevenly blurred. He suggested that they were most likely blinking on and off at different intervals. The photograph was also examined by an imaging specialist who works for IBM in Westchester County, New York. He stated that the lights are not incandescent, but rather result from an emission process. The lights actually represent different chemical elements being ionized, causing them to glow. The colors of the lights are very pure, much too pure to be the result of white light filtered through glass of various colors.

We showed the photograph of the UFO taken by David to many of the key witnesses who got a good look at the object on May 26. They all agreed that this was the object they had seen. Most of them were relieved that someone had gotten a photograph of it—proof that they did see the UFO. In the future, when they talked about it, people would not think that they were crazy.

The UFO Returns

On May 27, the giant, boomerang-shaped UFO reappeared over the skies of Newtown, Connecticut. The UFO was reported to have flown over the homes of at least 200 residents. People reported that the object was much larger than any aircraft and was very low in the sky. Some people said that a multicolored beam of light came out of the bottom of the object and engulfed some of the homes in the area. All the witnesses agree that the object was a boomerang or a semi-circle in shape, with at least twenty lights that were red, blue, green, white, and yellow, or amber. The object moved very slowly and for the most part made no sound, although some people said that they heard a faint humming sound like a finely tuned electrical motor.

One witness who had an interesting experience was Mr. Paul Dummas. We interviewed him and several of his family members at the 1988 Omega UFO conference, held at the Holiday Inn in North Haven, Connecticut. Mr. Dummas said that the object passed right over his home. He called his family to come out to see the object as it approached their home at about 9:30 P.M. The Dummas family ran out to the back porch just in time to see the object pass directly overhead. Mr. Dummas said that the UFO was so huge that when they looked up it just blocked out the entire sky—all they could see was this large object drifting right over their heads without a sound. "The object was so enormous that it took forever to pass over our heads, and it was no more than 1,000 feet up. This thing must have been at least two football fields long, and moved at a very slow speed."

Mr. Dummas then paused and said. "You're not going to believe this, but later that night a smaller object came back to my home at about three in the morning. For some reason I woke up and ran to the window, to see this object approaching my home. It was just a black thing behind a white cloud and it was moving closer and closer to my home. Then, all of a sudden, I found myself back in bed and thought it was all a dream. My wife told me she had a dream of seeing a bunch of little guys in a spaceship. I went to the bedroom of my two sons and found them both asleep, but when I moved them I was shocked to see that they both had bloody noses and the pillows were smeared with blood."

Mr. Dummas was quite upset about the entire incident He had heard speakers at the UFO conference talk about abductions and implants placed up the nose. We calmed him down and assured him that his experience did not necessarily mean that his family was abducted by aliens, and that sometimes there is a logical explanation for these events. Mr. Dummas brought his entire family to the conference to look for answers and to talk with people who are experienced in investigating UFOs, but all he found was more fear, which increased his trauma. We tried to follow up on this case, but for some reason the Dummas family declined to talk about their experiences any further.

On May 29 the object was seen once again crossing I-84, this time going to the northwest. A very interesting close encounter took place in the small Connecticut town of New Milford, which is about ten miles north of I-84. At about 10:00 P.M. Robert Nellis, a twenty-five-year old resident of the area, was in his car with his dog and his friend, Jeff. They were parked on a side road off of Route 7 in the northern area of New Milford, listening to the radio. They were exhausted; they had just completed a long day of boating on the Connecticut River. The dog began to bark and cry, at which point Jeff looked over to the northeast to see a number of lights hovering over some pine trees less than a quarter of a mile away. Suddenly, the lights began moving toward them and the car radio began to sound "funny;" strange-sounding static began to interfere with the station that they were listening to.

They continued to watch the lights move toward them. As the UFO got closer, they were amazed at the size of the object. They told us in an interview, "This UFO was at least the size of a football field." The dog continued to bark as the object passed over their car. Nellis looked up and saw a very dark structure that connected the lights and extended toward the rear of the object. He told us that the UFO was tear-shaped rather than circular, as they had first thought; the shape of the lights made it look like a half-circle. As the object passed overhead it was so huge that it blocked out the entire sky. The UFO was made of a very dark material with little reflectability. There was no sound, although it was no more than 500 feet above the car. After passing over their car the UFO then shifted towards the north. "We both saw some type of flashing light under the object that looked like strobe lights. One last thing: when the object left the dog was quiet, but when we first saw the UFO he was in the back of the car, and now he was in the front with us. I don't remember him jumping in the front and he is a German Shepherd, so I think I would have been aware of him doing that. I asked Jeff and he also doesn't remember the dog moving up to the front seat."

Both watched the UFO as it moved slowly toward the northwest. The total duration of the sighting was only ten minutes, yet there was a forty-minute difference between the clock in the car and their clocks at home. Stranger still, Jeff's wristwatch was also forty minutes slow; it showed the same time as the clock in the car. Mr. Nellis called Phil for several weeks after the sighting and told him that, since that night, he had felt "uneasy, restless and upset." He also told Phil that he was now afraid to go out at night and was even fearful about talking about his sighting because he knew "they" would be angry. When Phil asked him who "they" were he replied, "I don't know who they are, but I know they can hear me and they know what I'm doing." We lost track of both Robert and Jeff in 1990; we understand that both men moved somewhere out west.

The UFO that appeared over the skies of Connecticut during that time was no doubt under some kind of intelligent control, but who or what was this intelligence? Was it human, alien, or something even more fantastic. As in previous sightings, the object appeared to survey an area by projecting beams of lights onto the homes of residents. The UFO then returned to some of the homes of these people, and it seems that some form of contact may have been made.

CHAPTER FOUR ...

CLOSE ENCOUNTERS OF THE 4TH KIND

Over the past eight years we have investigated many UFO sightings in the northeastern United States. We were often asked by fellow ufologists if we had any cases in which people claim to have been abducted by the intelligence behind the UFOs. In other words, did we have any cases of a Close Encounter of the Fourth Kind?

Our response to most of these individuals was "no." Only to a handful of people did we admit that there were abduction cases, and plenty of them. This denial of such cases was at the personal request of the late Dr. J. Allen Hynek, with whom we had worked closely at the time. (Dr. Hynek and Phil Imbrogno were co-authors of *Night Siege: The Hudson Valley UFO Sightings*.) Dr. Hynek felt that UFO reports are hard enough to believe without adding the subject of abductions to the discussion. He wanted to concentrate on the hundreds of well-documented UFO sightings that were taking place in the northeast, especially in the Hudson River Valley area of New York.

With so many reports over the years and with the sightings still continuing, it was only a matter of time before the growing number of abduction cases, especially in the Hudson Valley, had to be dealt with. At the time this book is being written (1995), we have been contacted by at least 110 people who feel they have experienced far more than just a UFO sighting. Of the 110 cases, we feel that forty-two would be suitable for further study. Of these forty-two witnesses, twenty-two come from professional backgrounds. None of these people want any publicity. They have nothing to gain by reporting this type of experience.

We will explore four of the most interesting cases in this chapter and present our findings and conclusions. At the request of the witnesses, we have changed their names to protect them. All four cases took place in the Hudson Valley area of New York, in the same general location where author Whitley Strieber had his encounter. Strieber's story is documented in his best-selling book, *Communion*. Since the publication of *Communion*, many people have come forward with similar stories, people who otherwise would have kept silent. Those of us involved in UFO research owe Whitley Strieber a great deal of gratitude for coming forward with his experience.

A Mysterious Headache

On July 2, 1987, we received a call from a 36-year-old woman living in Toms River, New Jersey. We will call her Gail. She got our number after hearing us on a Newark radio talk show.

Gail sounded very troubled and insisted that she had to talk to us about a UFO-related experience she had undergone.

In late June, 1987, while she was lying down on her bed one evening, she began to feel uneasy, as if someone was watching her. The time was around 10:00 P.M., and she was alone. Her 17-year-old daughter was away visiting her father in Croton Falls, New York. As she lay on the bed she heard a voice say, "We have come for you...you will not be hurt." She was lying on her back, and realized that her entire body was paralyzed; she could move only her eyes.

Three strange-looking beings stood in the doorway to her bedroom. According to Gail, the three beings were dressed in something that looked like tightly fitting black jumpsuits. They stood in a single row, one behind the other. As Gail watched them in great fear, she noticed that the leader seemed to have a problem getting into the room. It was as if some type of invisible shield was blocking his way. He lifted his hands and pressed them against the invisible shield, as if measuring the extent of it. The light in the hall was dim, and Gail could not see their facial features clearly, but noticed that they were about five feet tall, with very long arms. The leader took some sort of rod from a side pocket in his uniform and turned the bottom of it. The rod glowed with a green light. After he passed it over the doorway area, the three beings walked into the room without any effort. As they entered the room, still in a single file, Gail noticed that they had large heads and eyes that looked like cats' eyes, but that extended around to the sides of their heads. She never heard them talk audibly, but realized that the leader was communicating with the other two because she perceived a variety of buzzing and clicking sounds in her head.

Gail tried to scream, but couldn't. She was only able to move her eyes. The leader placed himself on her right side, one of the other beings went to the foot of the bed, and the last one went to the left side of the bed. The beings on each side of her then placed their hands under her head and raised it up. Gail said that their hands were ice cold, like those of a dead person. All she wanted was for them to stop touching her skin, but she was helpless. She saw the one on the left take out a tube that looked like a narrow roll of white cotton. Then the being started pushing it up her left nostril. At that moment, she felt extreme pain in her head, and then started to lose consciousness. She remembers feeling as if she was falling from a great height, then her mind went blank. The next thing she recalls is waking up at eight in morning with a very bad headache. As she walked to the bathroom both nostrils started to bleed. She felt as if something was stuck up her nose, but nothing seemed to be there. She looked in the bathroom mirror and noticed that her nose was swollen and puffy. She also noticed a vivid rash on her neck and legs, and a mild rash on her arms.

Gail hoped all day that the experience from the previous night was nothing more than a bad dream. She did not want to believe it, and tried to block the entire episode out of her mind. When her daughter arrived home that evening, Gail began to tell her what happened, but before she even finished with her story, her daughter started shaking. She then revealed that on the same night, at about the same time, she and her father were followed by a UFO on Route 116 near Croton Falls, New York. She described to her mother a large, dark craft, triangular in shape, that paced the car for five minutes just above the treetops.

To say we found this report very interesting was an understatement. Croton Falls is near the border of Westchester and Putnam Counties in New York, and lonely Route 116 has been the site of more than one close encounter over the past five years. We also found it quite interesting that both mother and daughter, even though widely separated, had an experience with the paranormal at about the same time, both UFO-related.

Gail's rash and headaches continued for the next few days, then disappeared. Gail's story, however, does not end here. Several weeks later we received a call from her telling us that the entire experience had repeated itself. Gail told us, "Those creatures returned at the same time of the night, and they did the same exact things that they did before. It was as if I was watching a replay of the first time they came into my bedroom. They even had the same trouble getting into the room, and the leader once again took out the glowing rod." Her daughter was once again visiting her father. This time, however, she did not have any experiences.

There is more to this case than meets the eye. The daughter and father, according to our findings, may have had as much as thirty minutes of what ufologist and author Bud Hopkins calls "missing time:" that is, a time loss for which they could not account. Gail and her daughter continue to have UFO-related experiences to this day. Initial findings indicate that both she and her daughter may have a long history of interactions with the alien intelligence behind the UFO. These experiences may go back to the time of Gail's childhood, when she first told her mother that the little men would come through the walls of her bedroom and take her away. In many of the cases we looked into, we found that people who have repeated UFO sightings and contact experiences have had similar experiences during childhood. In some of these cases, generations of family members may have also been abducted or contacted by this intelligence.

The Night Terror

Route 116 in Croton Falls, New York, lies very close to Highway 684, which runs through most of Westchester County. The route is long and winding, and cuts through a heavily wooded area with a large reservoir off to one side. It has been the scene of many sightings in the past, and several claims of abductions by an alien intelligence. It was here that a young man had an encounter with something so strange that it totally changed his life.

The witness, whom we will refer to as Greg, was a 25-year-old computer scientist who lived in New Castle, New York. On March 13, 1988, at about 10:00 P.M., Greg was driving home on Route 116 from a friend's house in Croton Falls. Since the road has no lights, it is very dark at night. The reservoir was on his left and a wooded area was on his right. As he drove, he began looking to both sides of the road, because he suddenly felt uneasy, as if something bad was about to happen.

Greg noticed a number of very bright lights to his left, just above the reservoir. The lights seemed too low to be a plane, and appeared to be several hundred yards away. The pine trees along the road partially obstructed his view, so he continued to drive, but slowly. He came to a clearing, stopped his car, and noticed that the lights were still heading toward him. Greg then rolled down the window of the car and watched the lights as they continued to approach. To get a better look he pulled himself halfway out of the car through the window and sat on the car door. As the lights got closer, he saw that they were connected to some type of very dark structure. At that point he saw only four lights, in the shape of a semi-circle. There was no sound from the object and it was barely above the treetops. As the UFO passed over him, he looked up and saw that the object was triangular in shape and at least 100 feet from end to end.

The object was so large and low that it blocked out the entire sky. It moved so slowly that it took what seemed like a long time to pass overhead. Greg told us that the object only had lights in the front. The underside was in sections that had depth, and receded inward. Inside the recessed area he saw flashes of light. He compared these flashes with those of a strobe light. Then something strange took place. The next thing Greg remembers is that he was driving down the road and the object was gone. He does not remember getting back into the car, nor does he remember seeing the object completely pass over his car.

When Greg arrived home he found it very hard to sleep that night. For the next few days he would wake up in the middle of the night in a cold sweat, his heart pounding, feeling very confused. He knew somehow that these sudden episodes of night terror had something to do with the UFO he had seen. As the days passed, Greg found it very hard to concentrate on his work. He was also fearful of going out at night; he felt he might encounter the UFO again. For some time after the sighting he would wake up in the middle of the night and stare into the dark. He told us that he felt as if something was in the corner of the room, waiting for him to fall asleep so it could come and get him. This fear is not uncommon in cases like this. Witnesses feel a personnel connection with the UFO that they saw, and they feel strongly that it is out in the night, waiting for them. This feeling may actually be some kind of psychic connection with this alien intelligence, rather than simple paranoia, as we will discover later in this book.

We arranged to have Greg hypnotized by Dr. Jean Mundy, a certified psychologist and Professor Emeritus of Psychology at Long Island University. The result of the hypnotic session indicated that Greg had experienced an abduction, committed by the intelligence in the object that he saw on Route 116, sometime during his sighting. The time that Greg could not account for was revealed under hypnosis. The following is Greg's description of what occurred during that "missing time."

While the object was passing over his car, Greg somehow was drawn out of his car window into the UFO. The means by which this was done is not clear. Greg then found himself lying on a table in a dark room. There were several beings standing around him, and the being near his left side was moving some kind of instrument around his head. Greg tried to move, but every part of his body was paralyzed. Greg described the beings as short, with gray skin and round eyes. His description of the beings he saw is very similar to that in many of the reports we heard at that time, and to others that we received later. One of the beings then inserted something up Greg's nose, which caused him extreme pain. He felt as if "cotton" was being shoved up his nostril. While remembering this part under hypnosis, Greg began to cry out, and his nose began to get red and swell. Greg could do

Plate 4. Drawing of an alien that has been reported in many abduction cases. These beings are known as the "grays" and were very prominent during the 1962–1980 era of UFO history (composite drawing by.Ann Direnger).

nothing but lie there in pain and wait until the strange being completed his task.

After the insertion procedure was finished, Greg was allowed to get up. He was escorted by one of the beings at his side to what appeared to be a control panel. The being was short and only stood as high as Greg's chest (Greg is 5' 9" tall). At no time was there any spoken communication, but Greg knew where the being wanted him to go and what he wanted him to do. Greg was shown a panel composed of a grayish material that had "many projections" coming out of it. He thought they were controls that operated the ship. He looked around. Although the room he was in was dimly lit, he was able to see a corridor to his right that led to another room. The being then looked at him and he got a strong feeling that he was not allowed to go there, that this area of the ship was forbidden.

Then, without warning, Greg found himself back in the car driving home on Route 116. Greg feels that the being will someday come back for him, and that this time he will not be returned. His entire life has changed. He feels that he is now in some type of mental contact with the beings from the

UFO. He feels that he is gathering information for them, and that what he sees and experiences is somehow being transmitted to them. He told us that he did know that the beings come from a desolate planet, and that they envy us because our planet is so beautiful. Greg also told us that the beings can't understand why we are polluting our planet. They have a problem living here, but they are slowly adapting themselves, and future generations will be able to live in our environment. He told us that they do not understand our emotions. Greg feels he is being used by the beings so they can understand humans and how we react in different situations. For example, Greg may listen to music and he will then hear a voice inside his head say, "What is music? How does it make you feel?"

Greg's case is unusual, but not unique when compared with other cases we have investigated in the New York area.

The Missed Detour

The next case took place in 1984, during the peak of UFO and paranormal activity in the Hudson Valley. This episode involved a close encounter, missing time, and abduction. If this was a real experience, then the implications are fantastic. There is no doubt in our mind that the witness involved is not lying. He would have nothing to gain by relating his experience.

Bill, as we will call him, is a 32-year-old computer programmer for a major scientific/engineering corporation that helped design and build components for the NASA Hubble Space Telescope. On July 19, 1984, at about 10:30 P.M., Bill left work at his job in Norwalk, Connecticut. By 11:00 he was heading west on U.S. Interstate 84 just west of the New

York-Connecticut border. As he approached the turn-off to the Taconic Parkway in Dutchess County, he noticed a very bright, almost circular object in the northern sector of the sky. He counted about seven very bright, white lights that seemed to be just sitting there, not moving at all.

Bill slowed his car and tried to study the lights closely. This was difficult, since he was still driving and the lights were off to his right. They appeared to be moving to the left, and it was at this time that he noticed a dark mass behind them, silhouetted against the brighter, light-polluted night sky. He continued to drive west on I-84 and soon lost sight of the object. He tried to brush the entire sighting out of his mind, thinking, "Oh, it must have been those guys from Stormville airport flying those planes in formation, trying to fake a UFO." Bill thought this because previous sightings in that area had been explained away by federal and state authorities as being nothing more than a group of pilots flying stunt planes. This explanation, of course, was never proven to be the cause of the sightings that took place between 1983 and 1989. Bill continued to drive to his home in Dutchess county, listening to the radio as he went along.

At the Route 52 exit near Stormville, New York, he turned off and began travelling north. The time was now close to 11:15 P.M. and the roads were quite desolate. He came to a clearing where there was a field and noticed a large dark mass sitting about 200 yards from the road. At first he thought it was a new home, but then realized there couldn't be a house there. When he had gone that way just the night before, the field had been empty. In fact, Bill always drove home that way and there never had been any type of structure in this field before. Bill slowed down to get a better look. "This thing was huge and dark," he told us. "The strange thing was that it had almost the same shape as a long barn, the kind used for raising chickens, but it seemed more tapered toward the sides, and very smooth." As he watched, the dark object rose into the air without a sound. This really upset Bill, since his was the only car on the road. As it rose higher and higher, Bill could see that this was a very large object and very, very dark. It was now about twice as high as the trees. It slowly approached Bill, who was still in the car, now moving at a crawl. Bill's radio started to sound "funny," the voices and music distorted and out of tune. Bill told us that it sounded like the music out of a tape player with weak batteries. We found this comment interesting because radios, and all electromagnetic communications, will do this when subjected to a dampening magnetic field.

Bill got scared. He stepped on the gas pedal and sped away from the still-approaching object. His heart was racing almost as fast as his car as he drove up the road at more than fifty miles per hour. He lost sight of the object and slowed down, since he was in a thirty-five-mile-per-hour speed zone. After several minutes of driving he noticed a bright white glow over a hill ahead. As he approached the crest of the hill, he was shocked to see the object waiting there for him! It was about 300 feet above the trees and was all lit up with rows of white and yellow lights. Bill was sure this was the same object that he had seen earlier in the field, but this time the lights outlined a very large craft that seemed triangular in shape. Bill knew that this object was after him. How he knew this he doesn't know, but he felt it strongly.

Bill stopped his car and turned off the engine and lights. He was hoping that whoever was in the thing would not see him and go away. He felt very strongly that the UFO had tracked him and isolated him on the road and was now going to "capture" him. The UFO turned off all its lights, and Bill could see its large triangular shape hovering in the sky. The UFO then started moving slowly toward him, without a sound. As it passed directly over the car, he saw that it had quite a detailed bottom, with an intricate network of grids and strange circular areas that looked like portals. Bill told us, "I really don't want to make light of this, but the UFO looked like one of those star destroyers from the movie *Star Wars*. The underside was triangular, but I did not see the top of the craft, so I could not tell you what shape that was." As the UFO passed over Bill's car, he looked up and saw several circular areas that looked like tunnels leading into the object. Lights that looked like "strobe lights" were flashing inside these circular areas. Such circular, flashing areas have been reported time and time again during sightings of the close encounter kind. Bill estimated that this object was at least 300 feet long and more than 200 feet above his car.

The last thing Bill recalled was watching the UFO pass over the car. Then it was gone. The strange thing was that Bill did not see it fully clear his car—it just vanished! Stranger still, Bill's car was not in the same place as it was when he first saw the UFO. Bill and his car were now 600 feet down the hill he had driven up when he first saw the object. He was positive what time it was when he first saw the UFO. He was not positive what time it was when the UFO passed over his car, but felt it was about 11:30 P.M. The next time Bill took a look at his watch it was 12:30 A.M. The entire sighting from the moment he first saw the glow beyond the hill to the point at which the object passed over his car seemed to have taken no more than ten to fifteen minutes, yet according to his watch at least one hour had passed. Bill started to drive home, feeling very tired and uneasy. He also had a headache and a stiff neck—so stiff that it was almost impossible for him to drive.

When Bill arrived home, he told his wife about the sighting. She was already worried because he was more than an hour late. Later that night, Bill woke up screaming, "Get away from me! Get away from me! " His wife told us that since the night of the sighting he has been afraid to go out after dark. He even insisted that his boss keep him off the evening or night shift at his job.

The UFO experience and his dreams continued to torment Bill. He wanted to find out more, but it wasn't until 1987 that Bill contacted us and told his story. Bill had seen Bud Hopkins talk about alien abductions and missing time on a TV talk show. Bill asked us if it would be possible to have him hypnotized, so that he could find out what had happened to him during that lost hour of time. Hearing Hopkins talk on TV about the subject had frightened him. He wanted to make sure that he had not been abducted by aliens.

We arranged to have Bill meet with a local certified psychologist who occasionally performed regressive hypnosis. After a complete psychological work-up, our expert determined that Bill was sane, but had considerable psychological trauma because of a paranormal experience—in this case, a UFO sighting. The following is a transcript of Bill's session under hypnosis. He talked first about seeing the lights while driving on I-84, then about the dark object in the field. His voice at this point became filled with emotion and fear. We have edited out the hypnotist's questions and prompts.

"I see it now. It's that thing! It's coming over in my direction! I'm going to turn the lights off on the car so maybe they won't see me and they will go away. Its huge...oh, my God, what is it? There is someone standing in the road and he's walking toward the car. Who are you? I scream. He's says to me, 'Do not be fearful. We need you. You have been selected.' Selected for what!...Get away! I feel strange, like I am floating in air. It's all dark. I am now on this table and these guys are all around me. There are six of them. Two are at my head and two on the sides. My legs and arms are like dead weights. I can't move them".

Bill is then asked to describe the beings in greater detail.

"These guys are small. They have large heads with round black eyes, the eyes are so black...I can't see any pupils. They look like shark eyes, they don't even look real. They are dressed in some type of black and white skin-tight suits that look like diving suits. I can't see their hands, and the one that is near my head is moving some type of thing up and down the side of my head. It looks like a portable vacuum cleaner. He is moving it closer and it is making my head vibrate, it feels like a drill going through my head...STOP IT, STOP, IT HURTS! What are they doing to me? Will somebody please help me? This can't be real. They are looking for something and they found it. I can't hear them speak, but I know what they are saying. I can feel my legs and arms now and they are allowing me to get up. They are only up to the lower part of my chest and they are very skinny (Bill is 6' 1").

"The others are now over some type of panel. Two of them are leading me by the arms. They ask me not to look around and to keep my eyes straight...something about radiation from the sides of the ship hurting my eyes. Where are you from?...I don't understand...he said, we are from here. I am asking them if they are going to let me go...he said yes, but we shall see you again. He is telling me that they come from a place which is very ugly in comparison to ours and they would like to live here but they cannot. I'm telling him that I will remember everything and tell people what is going on. I told him that he just can't take a person like this and experiment with them because it's against the law. He is telling me that they do have the right to do it and no one is getting hurt. He is now telling me that I will remember some of what has taken place but there are forces which will stop me from telling others what happened."

Bill then found himself back in the car. Bill recalls every aspect of the experience, which to him was very real. To this day, he is still fearful that the strange creatures who abducted him on his way home will come back for him. During our investigation into Bill's case we were puzzled as to why there was no traffic on Route 52 that night. Although the population of that area is not as great as that of many other towns in the vicinity, Route 52 is a major road in Dutchess county. There should have been more cars on the road. Later we discovered that during the time of Bill's abduction the road was closed off, at least on one end. A motorist who traveled the road nightly said that as he drove off the exit ramp for Route 52 he saw a road block, with two or three men in coveralls waving cars to a side road detour. He couldn't get a close look at the men, but said they were in yellow outfits with hard hats. They were holding glowing rods rather than flashlights. Later we called the Dutchess and Putnam County road work crews and were told that no county workers were up there working at that hour of night. We also contacted the state highway crew, and the local electric, gas and telephone companies, but still could not find out who had blocked off the road. State police and local law enforcement also were of no help. Perhaps the road was blocked off by the intelligence in the UFO, the same beings who abducted Bill. Their purpose, without a doubt was to get him on that road by himself. What bothered us was that the people who blocked off the road were reported to be quite human-looking. We were to continue hearing reports like this one, in which human beings (or human-looking beings) were actually used to assist this alien intelligence in interacting with people in our society.

It is clear that the first three cases presented in this chapter have many similar features. As our investigation progressed we were to find more startling evidence that an unknown, possibility alien intelligence was at work with a definite hidden agenda. The final and last case that we will present in this chapter gives a hint as to what the purpose of these abductions might be.

We will present this case history without using the real names of the witnesses, even though we have their approval. In the past, many of the people whose names we used were constantly called and sometimes harassed by strange people, as well as by the merely curious. In some cases, so-called UFO investigators have shown up unannounced at witnesses' homes and barraged them with a multitude of questions.

A Double Abduction

Shawn was a 30-year-old construction worker who resided in Croton Falls, New York. Sally, his 32-year-old girlfriend, was also from the same area. On August 15, at about 2:00 A.M., they were driving to Mahopac on Route 6 after attending a party for a friend in a nearby town. As they drove, they noticed a glow off to the right that looked like a fire in the brush along one of the side roads. They turned off Route 6 onto Drewville Road and slowed the car. Shawn felt driven, almost compelled to check out the situation. Sally, on the other hand, had a bad feeling about the situation. She told Shawn that they should just go to the sheriff's office and report the incident to them. Shawn replied, "Look at that, it's like energy coming from the ground. We've got to check this out!" As he continued toward the fire he saw a number of flashing lights ahead, blocking the road. At first he thought that it was some type of fire or police vehicle, since the lights were blue and red. He stopped the car when he saw two figures walking toward him. Thinking at first that they were police, he got out of his car and took several steps toward the approaching figures. As the figures continued to get closer he thought that they were a little short, and then thought they might be kids fooling around. As they moved out of the glare of the lights he realized that they were not human. These creatures had large heads, long arms, and no hair. When the car headlights hit them, their eyes glowed red.

Shawn ran back, got into his car, and yelled to Sally to lock all the doors. He then told her to jump in the back seat and pull a blanket over herself, so that she could not be seen. Somehow he knew that they were after her, not him. The beings came right up to the doors and the front windshield of the car. Shawn told us, "It was as if they did not know how to work the handle on the car door. They kept on passing their hands over the front of the glass, expecting the door to open." He noticed that there were three of them now, one on the right, one on the left, and one in front of the car. He described the beings as less than five feet tall, with large, pear-shaped heads. He said that their eyes were huge and curved around their heads, looked almost like the eyes of an insect.

The beings continued to try to get in the car. Then Shawn started hearing "voices" inside his head. He knew that this was some kind of attempt at communication from the creatures. "They tried to get me to open up the door by convincing me that the lock is open in the down position. This almost worked. I started to pull the lock up, but I stopped. Then I looked at the front windshield and it began to melt in front of my eyes. I closed my eyes, looked again, and the windshield was all right. They tried to scare me out of the car by putting images of danger in my mind. I also had thoughts that the car was on fire and ready to blow up. I tell you, these beings did all this to try to get me to open the car door so that they could get us."

Shawn continued, "I knew that it was not me that they wanted; it was Sally. They knew that she was in the back of the car. It's strange, I did not hear her at all. It was as if she had fallen asleep in the back under the blanket. I then yelled out, now I don't know why I said it, but I yelled for them to leave her alone because she already had a hysterectomy. I then felt very light-headed, and the next thing I knew I was outside the car and Sally was nowhere in sight. I don't know how I got outside the car, but now there were six of those alien guys all around me in a circle. One came forward, and I thought he said that they were going to let me go when they finished this. I cried, and yelled for them to let me go, but this guy was very cold. It was like it was his job and no matter what I did, he was going to do what he had to. I felt like some type of specimen, and this was the Jacques Cousteau of outer space. The next thing I knew the sun was rising and Sally and I were back in the car parked along the side of the road. We didn't talk too much about what took place, and then about a week later we broke up. I haven't seen her in six months. When I called her at her job they told me they think she left the area, and I haven't seen her since."

Shawn would not agree to hypnosis or to see one of the therapists we work with. It is clear that Sally was abducted, and that this intelligence was very interested in her. We heard over and over again from many well-respected UFO researchers that some type of genetic experiments are being performed by this alien intelligence. Was this the reason they were so interested in Sally? Sally could never be reached by our investigation team. Shawn remains in the area to this day, convinced that he was abducted by aliens.

Although this story was a good one, and the witness was very honest and seemed to be telling the truth, as with most cases like this there was only one witness. We would later record several cases in which two witnesses were involved, but these are very rare.

The only way to make sense out of a case like this is to compare it with similar encounters from different parts of the world. This particular case also represents the first appearance of insectile or reptilian creatures in the northeastern United States. Until this point, most of the reports were of the gray or white aliens that are common in UFO literature.

CHAPTER FIVE

CONTACT

We have been investigating the UFO phenomenon for over eighteen years. With each passing year we have found that cases are becoming more complex and puzzling. It seems that with each question we answer, another twenty or so arise that we cannot answer. If this continues, we human beings may never understand the true nature of what the UFO phenomenon represents. There is no doubt in our minds that the UFO phenomenon exists, and that there is some unknown intelligence behind it. We have seen enough evidence in our own investigations to convince us of this. Who or what this intelligence is, and where it is from, are other major questions that need to be answered. There are many stories of people who claim to be in contact with some type of extraterrestrial intelligence. Some of these people channel information and actually preach to groups about the "true nature of the universe." It's strange that no two stories of these contacts are the same. If you get a number of these contactees in a room and let them talk for a while, they will all start arguing with each other about who is right. We feel that no contactees have any real idea about who is in contact with them.

In our early years of UFO research, we were satisfied with the theory that the entire UFO phenomenon could be explained—that these objects were nuts-and-bolts alien spaceships from another star system. Today, we feel that the evidence indicates that we may not be dealing with a physical phenomenon. It is our belief that a great number of UFO encounters are the product of contact with a non-physical life form. This life form can appear physical to us. It may also have considerable control over our minds and the way we perceive it. The UFO phenomenon is so complex that it can't be easily explained as visitors from another planet in fantastic spaceships. We think the truth is much more exotic than that. In fact, we would be disappointed if UFOs turn out to be something as simple as someone else's astronauts.

Most UFO contact encounters seem to be more like a psychic experience than a science fiction adventure. It may be that we do not perceive the true nature of the phenomenon. The UFO intelligence may exist in four dimensions and we, with our limited, three-dimensional senses, cannot see into their parallel reality. Where does this fourth dimension exist? Scientists tell us that the entire universe is layered in four dimensions. The fourth dimension exists in the same space as we do, but at a right angle to a right angle. If we could actually see in this direction, we would be able to peer into the four-dimensional universe. Since we can never see into this dimension we may never get a real perception of the true nature of the UFO phenomenon. The intelligence can continue to hide from us and interact with us without being detected. Another way to explain this is with the story of a child watching a magician perform a magic act. The child watches as the magician makes things appear and disappear. In reality, nothing is vanishing—it's all a trick. To the child who doesn't understand, it's all magic. Unless the magician shows the child how the trick is done, the child will never figure it out. It remains inexplicable in the child's eyes; it remains magic. We are like the child who cannot see all of the trick. We three-dimensional humans do not see the entire UFO intelligence, so to us it remains inexplicable, and we continue to search for answers that we may never find. This is why so much mysticism and religion has recently built up around the UFO experience. When we cannot understand what we experience we, like the child, assume that it must be magic.

UFO encounters can be classified into two categories. The first is a sighting of a UFO—a person sees something in the sky that he or she cannot explain. In most such cases, the sighting remains the only incident; the person just happened to look in the right place at the right time. Usually, the person is with one other person or a group of people and they all witness the same thing. The second type of encounter is a close encounter. Let us state that we do not believe that a close encounter with a UFO is an accident. Our studies have convinced us that experiences of this type are, in fact, cases of deliberate contact. Every witness we interviewed who had a close encounter sighting later had some type of contact experience, in most cases an abduction. In many close encounter cases, contactees believe they are being "probed," and that they can feel the presence of the intelligence in the UFO. There is no doubt that some kind of telepathic communication takes place during a close encounter. We call this a "contact" experience. Since contact experiences may take different forms, it is sometimes difficult to understand what type of contact the witness has experienced. Therefore, we have divided contact experience into five categories.

Close Encounter of The Third Kind. In this form of contact, the witness encounters a strange being near a UFO that has landed. In some cases no object is in sight. Usually the being looks at the witness, but no real communication is made between them. In a large percentage of the cases, the witness later has one of the other contact experiences described below.

Sighting of a UFO with Telepathy. In most UFO encounters, a person sees a UFO but feels nothing; there is only a sighting. In some cases, however, the witness feels a kind of psychic link with the UFO. The UFO seems to respond to the emotions of the person and, in rare cases, an actual thought is placed in the person's mind—a telepathic message from the intelligence behind the UFO.

Entity Communication. In this form of contact, the witness meets a human-like or non-human intelligence and has verbal or telepathic communication with it. In most cases the person is left with some sort of information; in rare cases no information is consciously remembered. Some encounters take place within or outside of a physical ship. In other cases, the entity appears at the person's bedside in the middle of the night. In one case on record, the witness claims that, on more than one occasion, an extraterrestrial being "popped" in while the person was driving, and engaged in a lengthy conversation while this person drove home.

Abduction. In these cases, people claim to have been abducted and taken on board a UFO, where they interact in some way with the alien intelligence that operates the craft. In most cases, some type of medical procedure is performed on the witness, and there is very little interaction between the alien intelligence and the person. In rare cases no medical or any other type of procedure is performed. Instead, the person is shown many wonders and given information about the universe and the beings that inhabit it.

Channeling. In this form of contact, a person claims to be in mental contact with a human, non-human, or super-human intelligence. Most communication is done verbally, through automatic writing, or with the drawing of diagrams. In many cases the person is taken over by the intelligence, but in some cases he or she is not. Most of the information seems to consist of useless philosophical statements about human nature that border on religion. In rare cases, actual technical information has been channeled; these are the cases that offer more data to study.

Extraterrestrial Channels?

The channeling phenomenon seems to be a new craze across the world. When we are approached by individuals who claim to be in contact with a super-human intelligence, our initial response is to put up the red flag. It has been our experience that the majority of people who claim to be channeling an extraterrestrial intelligence are in contact with nothing more than their own imaginations. Our research has established, to our satisfaction, that over 90% of these cases cannot be proved. The other 10% are interesting, but require the collection of much more data to find out what is really going on. While certain people may be in contact with an extraterrestrial intelligence, such cases are much rarer than various New Age publications would have us believe.

The scenario for channeling is the same in most situations. A channel (male or female) will sit in a chair in front of an audience and go into a trance. Then an extraterrestrial physical or non-physical entity takes over the channel's mind and body and begins talking to the audience. In some cases the voice of the person will change and an accent will appear. It's strange that the majority of people who channel start speaking with an Indian/Middle Eastern accent. The accent is rarely convincing; most of the time it sounds as if it's being forced—in other words, faked.

In New England, a channeled being named Elan has a very large following. Elan is an extraterrestrial who meets once a month or so with his group. The person who channels Elan goes into a trance, closes his eyes, then goes through a series of exaggerated, almost laughable, body motions as the being Elan enters the channel and starts to talk with the audience. The audience, most of whom are his followers, asks philosophical questions. Elan never gives a straight answer, but talks on and on, presenting lots of useless information without ever answering the original question.

When we asked Elan several scientific questions we never got a satisfactory answer. Instead, he gave us some long-winded metaphysical information. It seemed strange that a super-intellect such as Elan could not answer basic questions in astronomy than could be answered by any amateur astronomer. We don't want to appear negative about the entire channeling phenomenon, and we have become convinced that there is some type of contact going on. However, in many cases that we investigated, including that of Elan, the evidence is just not convincing.

Out of at least 125 case studies, the following are the only three that convinced us that the people involved might be in touch with an unknown, alien intelligence. A great deal of investigation has gone into these cases, which convinced us of the reality of the contact situation. All channeling may not be just dreams of fancy.

Contact from Solarian

When Phil first met Dean Fagerstrom in 1982, Dean was a 57-year-old resident of Putnam Lake, married with two children. He claimed to be in contact with a number of extraterrestrial-spiritual entities who used him to impart information to our world. Dean originally wrote a letter to Dr. J. Allen Hynek in 1981, describing his contact with a being called Donestra. Dr. Hynek was impressed with the letter because it was very well-written; its author was definitely intelligent, and seemed sure that what he was talking about was the truth. Dr. Hynek then sent Phil a copy of the letter and asked him to pay a visit to Mr. Fagerstrom.

We found Dean to be intelligent, articulate, and one of the most fascinating individuals we ever met in this area of study. Dean was the perfect host as we began talking about his contacts and how they took place. There was no hesitation on Dean's part. He talked easily about his experiences and seemed to trust us with the information. At no time did he behave as if he was uneasy. He began telling his story as if it were the details of his last vacation. It is very difficult to cover all the information that Dean told us, so we will present only the basics in this book.

Although Dean's contacts seem to date back to his childhood, his adult experiences began in November, 1966, while he was in the army, stationed at Bad Kreuznach, Germany. He lived downtown, about a mile from the base. One night at two in the morning, while sitting in his apartment, he began to feel strange, as if someone was in the house with him. The feeling of a presence was strong enough to make him get up and search around the house. Although the feeling was not threatening, he nevertheless felt some concern.

He returned to his desk, where he was working on a number system sequence to figure out the lottery. As he looked at the white board, a human-like face began to appear before his eyes. The face filled up almost the entire two-by-three board. As the image grew clearer, he saw that it consisted of not one face, but two. A bluish shimmer blurred the edges of the image. One face was that of a man, the other of a woman. The man had shoulder-length blonde hair; the woman's hair was slightly darker, and a little shorter. Both had piercing blue eyes. Dean was somewhat surprised by this apparition, but he felt no fear. He looked at the faces and they seemed very familiar to him. He knew that he had seen them before. He then heard a voice close to his ear. The male gave his name as Donestra. The female gave her name as Kilestra, and said that she was Donestra's wife rather than mate.

Donestra told Dean that they knew he had studied many things. They had been receiving his thought projections for years, because Dean's mind was a powerful transmitter. Donestra told Dean that the images he was seeing were not real, but were holographic projections. Donestra and his wife were among thousands of individuals from various planets throughout the near regions of the universe and beyond who had been studying Earth for many years. Donestra explained that our planetary and human condition interested them greatly.

After several minutes of conversation, the communication came to a close. Dean was asked not to mention to anyone what he had seen and heard. Dean was told to watch the skies in the next few days because he would be shown a sign the communication was true—not a dream. A few evenings later Dean was drawn to a window. He looked at the night sky and saw a huge object that performed amazing maneuvers. This sighting of an aerial ship was the evidence that Dean needed to prove that the contact had not been some late-night hallucination.

In 1967, after Dean was discharged from the service, he moved to Brewster, New York. His life was quiet, and the year went by uneventfully. Then on January 19, 1968, at 4:30 A.M., Dean had another encounter with an extraterrestrial intelligence, a contact encounter that changed the rest of his life. Dean woke up and saw a bluish shimmer in the upper corner of the room. He also heard an incredible, high-frequency buzzing sound. Gradually, an object materialized. It was about three inches in diameter, round, and resembled an old fashioned microphone.

This object came nearer and nearer until it halted before Dean's face at a distance of no more than a foot. This object was suspended in mid-air and continued to oscillate, producing a very high-frequency sound. As Dean watched, the device approach, something projected itself from the center of a disk and extended out four or five inches. The projection resembled an "ice pick;" it seemed to Dean that it was some type of probe. The probe came to within three inches of his forehead and started to emit a very intense vibration that shook his head and his neck. Dean lay helpless in bed for several minutes, until the device completed its task. The object then became quiet and vanished right before his eyes.

The next day, Friday morning, Dean got into his car and went to an art store. He bought graph paper, pencils, triangles, compasses, and various other types of drafting instruments. The buying spree did not seem to be under his control, nor did he understand why he was buying these things. Dean collected his purchases and went home. In less than seventy-two hours he made drawings of various types of "alien machinery." Dean did not know why he was doing this, but knew that Donestra had something to do with it. He had very little idea what the devices were that he was drawing.

The diagrams were done in a very unusual manner. Dean had no notion of what the final product would look like, but felt strongly motivated to complete the drawings. He would place a piece of graph paper in front of him and stare at it. After several seconds bluish dots would appear on the paper, showing him where to connect lines. He also seemed to have a pre-knowledge of what color or shade to place in a particular part of the diagram. Dean was instructed to name each diagram, but very little technical information was given. After the three days behind closed doors, Dean completed thirty-two diagrams (three reproductions of these diagrams appear in this chapter). As the years went by, Dean had continued contacts with Donestra. These resulted in Dean writing two unpublished, 500-page manuscripts, *The Book of Solarian* and *The Celestial Citizen*.

As we talked further with Dean about the information he obtained from Donestra, something very strange took place. He suddenly went blank and stood still for about forty-five seconds, as if he was in a trance. He then began to talk once again, and said, "He was here."

Phil replied, "Who was here?"

Dean said, "Donestra was here. He instructed me to turn the diagrams over to you. He said that you will know what to do with them when the time comes."

We found this very strange indeed. Dean completed the diagrams back in 1968. He held on to them for all those years and showed them only to a handful of people. Now, out of the blue, he handed the diagrams over to us and said, "You are the caretaker, now. They are out of my hands." We were very happy to get these drawings, because they were the first hard evidence that channeling might be more than pseudo-religious pipe dreams.

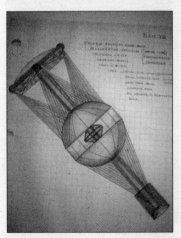

The diagrams are a marvel to behold. They are in vivid color, drawn with extreme precision. They have been examined by professional people from many different fields, who

Plate 5. Diagram of a telescope-like device channeled through Dean Fagerstrom from the being known as Donestra.

all have been fascinated by them. They have asked to meet the person who did them, and we would tell them we could arrange it. However, when we mentioned that they were done by an extraterrestrial being who is really an angel, we got some very strange looks. A professional draftsman said that a person would need at least twenty years' experience in drawing technical diagrams to produce them. He also said that a top-notch professional would need at least six hours to complete each diagram.

Many of the diagrams show devices that were unknown back in 1968, but are being experimented with today. One device is a three-dimensional viewing screen. Back in the late sixties this was science fiction, but today the prototypes for these screens on computers are now being used. There are also diagrams that show cold fusion, and a variety of optical test equipment and communication devices. There are diagrams showing propulsion systems that use photons (bundles of light energy), and a high-flux resonator for generating energy. One of the most interesting diagrams shows an atomic model of the hydrogen nucleus, showing that it is composed of as many as eight basic particles. If this is true it will

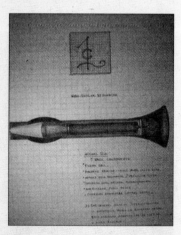

Plate 6. Another device channeled from Donestra through Dean Fagerstrom: a "High Flux Resonator." According to Dean, this device, when used on a human, can cause temporary paralysis.

change our entire concept of atomic physics.

Scientists at Princeton, Northwestern, and M.I.T. have also looked at the diagrams and agreed that they are accurate in design, although there is not enough information to tell you exactly what each device is, how it works, or how to build it. One device was called a Helical Coil. It seemed to be the most simple of the thirty-two designs. When this device was constructed, it pro-

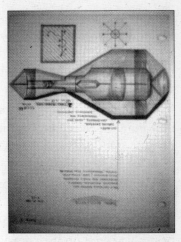

Plate 7. Donestra channeled this diagram through Dean Fagerstrom. This device is called a "Photon Accelerator."

duced an electromagnetic flux much greater than can be produced by any similar coils available today. The only problem was that, after a short time, the coil burned out and the device stopped functioning. An iron core was used in building the device; when we mentioned this to Dean, he seemed to think that the metal core should have been constructed with some kind of magnesium alloy.

If the diagrams weren't enough of a mystery, Dean then produced several pages of writing in an unknown language. The symbols were examined by an expert in linguistics. It was his opinion that the symbols were not gibberish, but a complex language composed of over 200 characters. He stated that the language resembles ancient Babylonian, but as far as he could tell the symbols were indecipherable. Accompanying the text is a short poem, in English, called, "Out Of Orion's Mouth." Below the English words are symbols. Perhaps this is a sort of Rosetta Stone that will someday be used to interpret the symbols. We wonder what these symbols mean and what secrets they hold.

Dean seems to have a super-charged mind. He is capable of a number of fantastic mental feats. Dean claims that one night at 3:00 A.M., he woke up to see three little hooded beings enter his room. He was not frightened, but he could not move. The beings proceeded to perform some type of surgical procedure, and removed the top part of Dean's skull. He saw them put several small, ruby-colored crystals into his brain. Then the beings gathered up their small surgical pack and left the way they came. Since this time Dean has been not only a math genius, but also capable of performing extraordinary pieces of music on the piano.

Dean had yet another fantastic story to tell us, about another experience that profoundly changed his life. On the evening of April 26, 1985, Dean was on his way home when a detour sent him out of way and he became lost. Driving around, trying to find his way back, he ended up at the New

Plate 8. A sample of the unknown symbols that Dean Fagerstrom produced while under the influence of Donestra. It is a language of at least 200 characters, and resembles ancient Sumerian.

Fairfield High School. As he was turning around in the parking lot an object in the sky caught his attention. He stopped to look at it and saw a craft coming toward him at a thirty-degree angle, moving very slowly. He felt very apprehensive, but only because it was moving toward him. He doesn't remember opening the car door—it simply opened, and he got out without thinking about it An aqua-green tunnel projected toward him from the ship, winding like a culvert. A pilot, a very good-looking fellow, stepped out of the tunnel, chuckling, and told Dean that he had nothing to fear.

The man, dressed in a burgundy flight suit, instructed Dean to follow him. They entered the ship, which departed at a good rate of speed, although there was no sense of motion. There were elongated portals to look out of, but for whatever reason Dean didn't use them.

They arrived at an earthlike place. It was dusk, and a couple of buildings were visible. The pilot informed him that he was going to one of the buildings, but Dean was to walk straight forward and would be shown what to do. Dean walked toward a building and began to climb steps. Then, without warning, Donestra appeared out of nowhere, right in front of him. He was dressed in the same manner that Dean always saw during his telepathic communications, in a one-piece blue jumpsuit.

Donestra instructed him to go over to a building and undress, then enter a cubicle. He would know what to do. Dean did as he was instructed. When he entered the cubicle, a liquid more dense than water covered him and cleaned him. Water rinsed the other liquid off, then suddenly he was dry. When he emerged from the cubicle, his clothes were warm and looked as if they had been to the cleaners.

Donestra explained that he had to be cleansed from internal ideas, then took him to a large stone table where five beautiful girls representing five races were talking and laughing. Dean wanted to talk to them, but Donestra said the time was not right. He told him a few more things that Dean wasn't allowed to tell us. Donestra made a familiar gesture as he left—the same hand gesture that Dean's father made the last time he saw him. Dean returned to the craft, the pilot came back, and Dean doesn't remember any of the return voyage. He ended up in his car with the door closed. He could see the craft hovering above a nearby lake. When he got home, his son was really worried, for he was over two hours late.

Over the years Donestra taught Dean quite a few things about the universe and the purpose of the human race. Donestra told Dean that our universe is merely a projection of a much larger universe that is composed mostly of energy. This other universe has been known as the "spirit world" or "other side" and exists on many different levels. Donestra himself is a sort of angel who once lived in our universe. Donestra was born on June 19, 1647, on a planet called Solarian. He left our universe (died) on July 26, 1776, at the age of 129 years. He is one of three highly placed individuals with a special mission.

This was the first time that we encountered a contactee who claimed to be in communication not with just an extraterrestrial, but an ET who died and became an angel!

Another one of the three highly placed beings made an appearance to Dean on New Year's Day, 1989. This being is also a sort of angel, older and more powerful than Donestra. You might say he is Donestra's boss. The being told Dean that his name was Aphax and that he was once a priest in ancient Thebes. He taught philosophy and math in the year 2334 B.C. Dean was then taken out of his body and brought to ancient Egypt, where he saw a magnificent stone building. He approached the building, saw a small opening, and looked into it. He could see a sarcophagus laid on a table; the profile on the lid was of a person unknown to him. As he watched, the sarcophagus disappeared and was replaced by the image of his father. He continued to watch, and saw his father's image disappear and he himself lying on the table. He hoped that Aphax could explain what he was seeing. To his surprise, Aphax had turned into a stone statue and seemed to be part of the wall. At that moment, numbers and equations started pouring into Dean's head. Aphax instructed him to resurrect a lost numerical code that would explain events in the universe that have taken place in the past, are taking place in the present, and will take place in the future.

Dean showed us some of these equations. They are impressive, to say the least. Dean uses these numbers to help him understand the information that is given to him by Donestra and Aphax. He also uses this numerical system to help him win the lottery, although it only works to help him get the things that he needs to carry out his studies and communications with Aphax and Donestra.

So far, everything that Donestra and Aphax has instructed Dean to do has worked out well. None of it has brought any harm to Dean; on the contrary, it has all been beneficial in some way. As we mentioned before, Dean has become a musical genius, playing astounding pieces on the piano. Donestra explained that the composer Franz Listz, an Austrian who lived from 1811 to 1886, would play through him. Dean was instructed to go out and buy an electric piano, which he did. He really didn't understand why, since he doesn't play the piano. While we were there on our last interview in August of 1995, we asked Dean about his playing. He said, "I only play to record the music and I can only play it once." We had listened to some of his recordings; they were incredible. Phil got a copy of one and had an expert pianist listen to the tape. The expert recognized it as the style of Franz Listz, but it was a piece he had never heard before! It seems that Dean is composing new works by a master composer who has been dead for over 100 years. Recently, Dean claimed that Listz himself appeared before him and told him that he was to use his music to help stir feelings in those who will listen.

We continued to press Dean about his playing. While we were standing there, he suddenly sat down and started to play a beautiful, complicated piece of music. We were both dumbfounded. We were watching a man who has never had a music lesson in his life, who can't read music, playing an incredible musical score. We stood in awe as he played it out. When he had finished, we couldn't help but ask what had happened. Dean explained that occasionally he can play pieces from the larger composition by remembering where the keys are. But his performance was much more than a memorized trick. He showed all the feelings of a master player, allowing the emotions of the music to come through. To date, Dean has recorded almost two hundred different compositions, all of them channeled by Listz, all astounding.

It is very hard to find a rational explanation for the Dean Fagerstrom case. We invite any skeptic or interested person to contact him. You can reach the authors using the address given in the front of this book. If you state why you would like to speak with Mr. Fagerstrom, we would be most willing to help you contact him.

The Master

The next contact case is somewhat different, in that the outcome was not as positive as in Dean Fagerstrom's experience. This case involved a middle-aged man who was, at the time, a special investigator for the Department of the Treasury. Since his position was sensitive we will not use his real name, but will refer to him as "James."

We received a call from James in November, while he was living in Newton, Massachusetts. He told us that he had photographed a UFO while it was hovering outside his home, and that it had been witnessed by at least a dozen others. We were impressed with his story. As an investigator for a government organization, his recollection of the facts was excellent.

We met James at his home and he began to tell us about the sighting. On November 10, at 10:00 P.M., he witnessed a brilliant yellow, egg-shaped object in the sky. The object was much brighter than any of the stars, but not as bright as the moon. The object would hover, then make fantastic figure-eight movements in the sky. The object moved so fast that at times it looked like an illuminated "8." When the object hovered it emitted a reddish glow around its edges and ejected a spark-like material that looked almost like fireworks. James told us that he was the one who alerted his neighbors that something strange was in the sky. This was the fifth time that the UFO appeared in the sky that month.

James seemed to feel when the object was about to be seen, so this time he had a camera ready, and a telescope, in the hopes of capturing a close-up photograph of the strange aerial visitor.

We were very interested in the fact that James was able to predict when the object would be seen, but for the moment we just sat back and listened. As he continued to talk and began to take us in his confidence, we realized that this was much more than a sighting of a UFO. It was indeed a contact case, and a very bizarre one at that.

James showed us the photographs (color slides) of the object that he had taken through his small telescope. He then showed us how he took the pictures. He would take his small refracting telescope, supported on a flimsy tripod, hold his 35mm camera near the eye piece, just point the telescope toward the part of the sky where the UFO was, and he then start snapping photographic frames. At no time did he ever focus, nor was the camera physically connected to the telescope. He was using a 9mm eyepiece, which gave him a magnification of over 100 power.

After we heard his story and saw the method with which he took the photographs, we asked to examine the slides. The slides showed an egg-shaped object. The image was not blurry, but very sharp. We are both accomplished astrophotographers and the telescope is no stranger to us, so when we looked at the slides we were both surprised at their clarity. Under ordinary circumstances, there is no way that James could have gotten images that sharp with the method he was using. The slightest vibration would cause the image to blur—yet the image of the UFO on the color slide film showed no blurring at all. Although it was just a light source, it looked like a glowing solid object. At that point it was hard for us to accept James' story, but it was verified by a number of witnesses, including several of his neighbors, the town minister, the zoning commissioner, and the Postmaster. Once again we must make it clear that the way the photographs were taken is theoretically impossible!

We then had to come to grips with the fact that perhaps the image of the UFO was placed directly on the film. It would not have mattered if the camera was pointed in the other direction, the image would still have been placed on the film in perfect focus. We have seen examples of psychic or paranormal photography done this way, but in this case there was a photographic record of a visual anomaly. If this was the case, then it would mean that some intelligence, possibly alien in nature, placed the image on the film so that it could be seen—but for what purpose?

There have been many cases in which people have tried to take pictures of UFOs, only to have their film come out blank. Yet there are some very clear and interesting-looking UFO images on film, video tape, and motion picture film. Why do some photographs of UFOs come out, while others do not? We can discount a small percentage of cases; some people do not know how to use a camera. However, the incidence of photographic failure is much too high for this to explain all the cases. We were once told by a UFO contactee that the only pictures we have of them are the pictures they allow us to have. In the case of James, it seems that this alien intelligence wanted us to have a photographic record of its nighttime visitation over the Massachusetts skies.

During our next meeting with James, we told him our findings concerning the images on the film. He assured us that

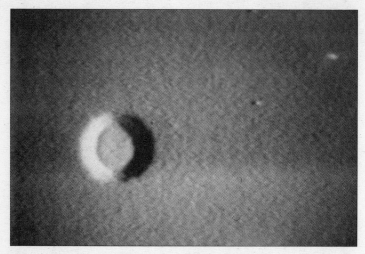

Plate 9. Computer study of the Newton, Massachusetts UFO photograph taken by James. Computer analysis proved that the photo was not a hoax; it really shows a solid object, thirty feet in diameter and at least one mile from the camera. This computer frame shows the true structure of the object.

they were not fakes. He then became very uneasy and told us, "I am going to tell you something very strange and incredible, but for the moment I don't want it to leave this room." James then started telling us the reason why he knew the UFO would appear and why he knew that he would be able to take the pictures of the object under impossible circumstances.

He explained that he was in mental contact with a being from another universe. He also said that this being arranged for the UFO to be seen and the photographs to be taken to prove that James was not crazy. Phil then pushed James to tell him the name of the being. After some hesitation, James replied, "He is known as the Master Surgeon of the Universe." James then started relating some of the information given to him by the Master Surgeon of the Universe.

James was told that he was contacted from a very early age, and was selected to bring information to the human race from the "Master's people." Although the being never told James exactly where he was from, he did tell him that he was part of a race that was non-physical. They were entities of energy, existing in another dimension. The Master then told James that they were responsible for the human race and were now trying to straighten things out; we are an experiment that went wrong. They were doing this by contacting certain people, like James, and giving them information to help our world.

James had been in contact with the being on a mental level for several years. He never saw the Master in person. The communications became more frequent after the photographs were taken. The Master would wake James up at all hours of the night to "talk," and to give him information about future events and UFO sightings all over the world. Needless to say, this became a major concern for his wife and two children, who witnessed James having conversations with thin air. James soon learned that he did not have to talk, because the Master could read his thoughts. Soon all of their conversations were on a mental level, with James mentally hearing the questions and answers provided by the Master. However, the information that was given to James never really checked out. For example, very late one night James called Phil to tell him that there were going to be massive UFO sightings over France and major earthquakes and natural disasters within a week, but nothing took place.

The communications became so frequent, they started interfering with James' job as a government investigator. The Master would start to tell James that he was going the wrong way when driving, which resulted in James getting lost and going on a wild goose chase for hours before reaching his destination.

One night the Master told James that there was going to be a landing of a ship in Connecticut—they were going to meet face to face. James got into his car in the wee hours of the morning and began driving to a location that was given to him. He really did not want to go, but by now he knew that if he disobeyed the request, the Master would torment him all night and not let him sleep.

James drove in circles for an hour, until the Master directed him to a dirt road and fenced area just outside Sandy Hook, Connecticut. James was instructed to climb the fence and he did so, ignoring the "No Trespassing" signs posted around the perimeter. After he climbed the fence, he walked in a field and saw some structures and huge antennas ahead. He continued to walk until he heard a noise and was blinded by a brilliant white light. The light was so bright that he could not see anything, so he stood motionless, waiting to find out who this was. He called out, asking if the light was the Master—but it was not.

James had been stopped by a military security patrol. It seems that, with the Master's help, James stumbled upon a government installation that we later found out was partially operated by the National Security Agency. James was arrested for trespassing. When they found out that he was a government employee, they called his supervisor to come and get him the next day. When James told his fantastic story about his communications with the Master, he was forced to get psychiatric help and was placed on several drugs. James told us that when he started taking the drug the communications with the Master stopped, but he can still feel his presence. He knows that if he does stop taking the drug the communications will continue where they left off.

James' case is bizarre, but not unique. We believe that he actually did experience some type of extraterrestrial contact. The photographs he took speak for themselves. They clearly indicate that some other force or intelligence was at work. There are hundreds of contact cases, but very few of them produce results that can be researched. In James' case, he has the photographs and he found a secret NSA tracking station.

The Unexplained Chill

Several years ago we received a letter from a couple who at the time lived in Greenwich, Connecticut. The letter stated that they had been channeling several extraterrestrial entities and wanted to know if we would like to be in on one of their sessions. The letter went on to say that they were in contact with not one, but 104 different types of ETs, all belonging to a sort of federation of planets. The couple's real first names are Mark and Lois; as in many cases, we prefer not to give their last name. Both are professional people, and it is our policy to protect the identities of those who confide in us, unless of course permission is given to use the full names of the witnesses.

Mark and Lois had been channeling these extraterrestrials for over a year through automatic writing. Mark worked as a manager of a major company in Greenwich, while Lois was a professional musician. Phil made an appointment to meet with them in their home that December. He was not sure what he would find. Accompanying Phil to the meeting was George Lesnick, a fellow researcher and a police officer with over twenty years of experience and a great interest in UFOs and paranormal phenomenon.

Phil and George arrived at the home of Mark and Lois and were greeted by the couple and their dog, a mixed Shetland collie, a very friendly and gentle dog. Everyone sat on the couch and tried to get to know one another a little better before Phil began his routine questions. George was preparing everything so that as much information as possible could be obtained that night, but nothing prepared us for what was to take place in the next several hours.

Phil started to ask about their contact experiences, but at that moment they were joined by a young woman. Mark and Lois explained that she was a gifted psychic. She was interested in their communications, and often sat in on their channeling sessions. The method of communication was simple. Lois would hold a pencil and paper on her lap and Mark would touch her hand lightly. Lois would then feel what to write on the paper. At times, her hand would move by itself, apparently under the control of the entity. This procedure is called "automatic writing" It was very popular at the turn of the century during the spirit craze, when thousands of people spent countless hours trying to talk to those who had passed on to the other side. Now the procedure was being used not to contact spirits, but to communicate with aliens on other worlds and in other dimensions.

The communication would not take place if Mark did not rest his hand on Lois' wrist. They said that the combination of the energies of both of them provided the power for these extraterrestrial to communicate. Phil asked if this was the only method of communication and Mark replied, "Yes, but they promised to channel voice information through one of us in the near future."

Everyone sat in a sort of circle as the couple attempted the communication. Lois' arm began to twitch. Mark, feeling this tension, stated that contact had been made with one or more extraterrestrials. As soon as the communication began the dog, once friendly and gentle, became very nervous, almost vicious. The dog had a strange glare in her eyes as she watched George and Phil. Every time they moved she would look at them and growl. Before the communication, the dog's eyes were gentle and soft, but now they were glaring and a very angry, deep black. They also seemed to glow in the dim light of the room, and the hair on the dog's back was standing up. There was no doubt that the communication was some-how affecting this animal in a very negative way.

As the communication began Mark asked, "Who is in touch with us tonight?" The following beings then began "signing in." Some of them were frequent visitors, with whom Mark and Lois were very familiar, while others were beings that they hardly ever heard from. These beings are listed below, with a brief description of who they are and, in some cases, where they come from.

Monka: A sort of priest-philosopher who resides under-ground in the pyramids of Mars. He is also called the "Protector of Earth." Monka is not a physical being, but a being of energy who lives in another dimension on the Red Planet.

Fanta One: Not much was said about this entity, although we did learn that Fanta One was not one individual being, but at least fifty, who work together and belong to a federation of planets.

Nemus: A high-ranking technical scientist from this federation of planets.

Soltec: A sort of mystic priest.

Wan: Resides in the core of the Earth. Home planet is called Lumina in the Andromeda galaxy. He is a nuclear physicist.

Han: Wan's mate, who lives with Han in the core of the Earth with their 5-year-old son, Eot. Han is an endocrinologist.

Lomu: An artist from the Lomu system. Channels sketches to Mark and Lois at least once a week.

Zar: A healer or doctor from the Lumina system.

Kalira: A politician or leader from the Lumina system.

Urso: A military leader and captain of a giant ship that often visits earth. Origin was unknown.

The channeling sessions all began with Monka greeting us with the words, "In the Light of the Radiant One." Most of the communications that came through offered no value to Phil as a scientist. The beings steered tactfully away from hard-core scientific questions. They were more concerned with teaching us about philosophy and New Age ideas. If a question was asked about science, either Han or Nemus would answer. If a question was posed about religion, then Monka or Soltec would answer. If a diagram was needed, Lomu would take over.

The actual content of the communication is not important at this point. What is important are the physical manifestations that began to take place. Five minutes after the communications began, the temperature of the room began to drop. Before the session, the temperature was seventy-six degrees. As the communications began, it dropped to fifty-six. Although heat was blasting out of the furnace vent and the thermostat was turned up to eighty-five degrees, the temperature of the room remained cold, and as the night went on it continued to drop. After a while the air became so cold that you could see your breath. George remained motionless in a chair, his eyes closed, for at least ten minutes. At first Phil thought he was resting, but later George had no recollection of his black-out. The young psychic woman complained of a great deal of pain in her head and also drifted off into a semi-conscious state. She became so ill that a friend had to come for her and take her home. The dog also reacted to what was going on—in fact, the dog seemed terrified.

Some force in the room was draining energy. Everyone except Phil seemed affected by it. As the communications continued a warning came, through Monka, that a negative being, a very powerful, evil force, was trying to destroy Phil because he was coming too close to discovering the being's true identity. During the session the phone rang, but no one was on the line. There was a strange knocking on the window, and a number of unusual sounds that resembled low chanting were heard. It was difficult to say whether the chanting came from outside, or from another room. When Phil asked the being Soltec if he could manifest something in the room, a tea pot flew off the kitchen stove and crashed to the floor, making a very loud noise.

As strange as all these incidents seemed, the communications with Monka and his group then took an even more bizarre turn. As Lois was writing the information received from Monka, her hand began to vibrate, as if she was losing control. She and Mark were not expecting this; they displayed surprise—almost fear. Without warning, a message arrived from another source. A brief transcript of the exchange is provided below:

Mark: Who is this, please?

Unknown Being: I will speak only to Phil.

Phil: Well, can you tell me who you are?

Unknown Being: Donestra.

Phil was amazed. This was, without a doubt, the same Donestra with whom Dean Fagerstrom claimed to be in contact. There was no way that Mark and Lois could have known about Phil's contact with Mr. Fagerstrom, or about the diagrams that Donestra had instructed him to turn over to Phil.

Phil: Donestra, what the hell am I supposed to do with these diagrams?

Donestra: In time you will know. You must, however, be warned that a very ancient, evil force has been trying to get to you for a very long time. You and the being are old enemies, for you have defeated him many times in the past. I cannot hold this line of communication.

Donestra then faded out, and Monka and the rest of the others returned.

Nemus, Fanta One, Wan & Lomu: Who was that? I think he had trouble getting through.

Monka: He is a very high order of being. He used me as a medium to channel that information through Lois so that Phil could get it. I have never encountered this before. I must find out more information and must end this communication session now.

At that point the session ended. Everyone except Phil was exhausted. It seems that Donestra had used Monka to channel information to the group—something no on had expected. When the channeling session ended, the temperature of the room began to return to normal. When Phil got out of the chair he felt a blow from some invisible force. He experienced a great deal of pain in his lower back, as if someone had just shoved a fist into his kidney. During the next few days the pain was so bad he could barely walk. As George and Phil left the home of Mark and Lois, the dog was once again friendly. George was so taken aback at what had occurred that he gave up researching the paranormal shortly thereafter.

The story does not end here. In the months that followed, Phil visited Mark and Lois again, but after that first night the communication was never quite the same. Monka almost refused to channel any information when Phil was present. The reason for Monka's reluctance is not known, but there was one indication that Donestra was involved. Donestra's name continued to pop up in our research as the years went by. We still don't know exactly what happened at the home of Mark and Lois that night, and we aren't 100% convinced that Monka and his gang really exist. However, what took place cannot be explained in any ordinary terms, so we ask our readers to keep an open mind.

Recently, a new channeling group invited us to a session. This group consists of people who gather in a Connecticut home to contact a number of extraterrestrials who call themselves the "Ring." The Ring is supposedly another federation of planets whose members try to impart wisdom and information to the "underdeveloped beings of planet Earth." Although the Ring sessions, and those of groups like the Ring, are harmless and filled with concepts of goodness, we can find no evidence that such groups are in contact with an extraterrestrial intelligence.

In one session with another popular group, called the "Gathering," the extraterrestrials promised to channel a number of diagrams that would allow us to build a device with which we could communicate with them directly. Weeks passed, but no diagrams were channeled through the group. At Phil's final session with the group he asked about the diagrams. The answer was, "We will be sending them within the next six months, but you have to be at all the sessions to learn more about the true nature of the universe." At this point Phil lost his patience and said, "Why do I have to wait all that time? And why does the information have to be channeled? There is no guarantee that I will be able to build this device. Why don't you just come down here in one of your spaceships, drop it off somewhere, and I'll pick it up? Think of all the time that will save." Well, that was the wrong question to ask. Soon after Phil spoke, communications ceased abruptly. He was never invited to another channeling session with the Gathering.

CHAPTER SIX ...

NIGHTTIME VISITATIONS

I n 1984 Phil was invited to speak at the annual conference of the Mutual UFO Network (MUFON). Twelve speakers were present, but his paper was the longest, as it covered the Hudson Valley UFO sightings from 1982 through 1984. Since the conference was held in San Antonio, Texas, Phil flew down from New York and met Dr. J. Allen Hynek at the hotel where the conference was being held. Dr. Hynek had also been invited as a speaker. Dr. Hynek and Phil had worked closely together many times in the past, not only on matters related to the UFO phenomenon, but also on astronomy. Phil was asked to attend a closed meeting with Dr. Hynek and a number of prominent scientists who were also attending the conference.

Phil felt quite honored to be invited to this meeting, which was closed to most of the UFO investigators attending the conference. Although Phil was still a well-known science educator with a strong background in astronomy, he felt quite out of place during the meeting. Some of the greatest minds in the country, including several Ph.D.s in a variety of fields, had gathered to discuss the UFO experience. Phil recalls, "It felt strange sitting there. At the time, I had only a Bachelor's degree and was working for my Masters. Most of what was discussed was way over my head, because it involved equations and theories that I'd only heard rumors about."

The topics that were covered in that six-hour meeting changed the way Phil looked at the UFO phenomenon for the rest of his life. They provided the basis for all his future research, not only in the UFO phenomenon, but in all areas of the paranormal. The discussions centered on the possibility that the UFO phenomenon may be dual in nature. That is, we may not be looking at something simple like spaceships, but at something more complex. The general feeling at the meeting was that the phenomenon was multi-dimensional and capable of fantastic manipulations of matter and energy. The scientists present, including Hynek, felt that the UFOs were from another dimension, and that they used this method of multidimensional travel to traverse not only the galaxy, but perhaps the entire universe.

During the meeting equations were presented that showed the existence of this four-dimensional universe—a strange place indeed! This is a place where time itself stands still, a place where the past, present, and future exist together. Surely intelligent beings who could enter this four-dimensional state could travel back and forth in time and cross great distances in an instant. From our point of view they would be able to disappear, reappear, and appear to change shape. Dr. Hynek presented one case that he was currently investigating, involving a pilot who, while flying over New York, encountered a large, unknown object approaching from the west.

A Black Rip in the Sky

The pilot grew very concerned. He got on his radio and called the FAA radar control tower in Islip, Long Island, and asked for the identification of the large aircraft to his northwest. The pilot was told that there was no air traffic in his area. Since he was flying a small twin engine plane, the pilot decided to keep as much distance as possible between his plane and the unknown object. He was concerned that it might be a large 747 or C-5A; if it was, he could easily get caught in the backwash of the jet engines. The time was about two in the afternoon and, since it was in June, the sun was still very high in the sky. Although the sun was shinning right on the object, it looked jet-black, "like there was a black rip in the sky," the pilot said. The object continued to approach. This is when he noticed that it was boomerang in shape. It was unlike any aircraft he had ever seen, and was at least the size of a C-5A, which is the largest aircraft used by the United States military.

No matter how many times the pilot changed his course to get out of the path of the object, the UFO always kept in front of his plane, and kept getting closer and closer. He started to get very worried, then just plain scared—it looked like the unknown object was on a collision course with his plane.

Dr. Hynek then played an audio tape of his interview with the pilot. It was clear from the pilot's voice that he was still upset about the entire incident, as well as a little uneasy to be talking about it to a scientific researcher. A transcript of the pilot's sighting account is presented below:

"It was no more than a half mile away and was slowly moving toward me at about the same speed and altitude as my plane, which was about 8,000 feet at that time. I thought for sure that it was going to hit me when all of a sudden the thing just folded in on itself and turned into a thin, dark line, then vanished with a flash. The only thing that I could compare it with was like when you have a telescoping antenna and you fold it down to this small thing—well, that's what this thing did, except it disappeared. When my plane passed through the area where the UFO had been there was quite a bit of turbulence for about two or three seconds. As I continued on to Westchester County Airport, I saw four F-15s fly by at about 15,000 feet and circle the area twice. When I landed, I expected to be greeted by the military or the CIA or something, but nobody came, so I just parked my plane and went home and decided not to report it."

This was a sighting of the Hudson Valley UFO. Dr. Hynek was extremely interested in this report because he had just returned from the New York area, where he and Phil had spent several weeks researching that series of sightings. All present at the meeting felt that, in order for a large object like this to disappear, it must have entered the fourth dimension. Although this would make it appear as if it vanished, the object did not disappear; most likely it was still in the same space as the plane, but in a different time, or on a different level of existence.

At this meeting, not only the sightings of UFOs, but also abductions were discussed. Most of the scientists present were against trying to publicize the abduction reports because they were very hard to believe at the time. In 1984 the idea of a simple UFO sighting was hard enough for most people to accept; the fact that some people claimed to have been abducted by an alien intelligence was just too much for that time. Nevertheless, abductions were brought up and current case files discussed. Everyone present seemed interested in the typical abduction scenario, that is, a close encounter with a UFO, followed by a certain amount of missing time that cannot be accounted for (usually about one to three hours), during which the person is taken aboard some type of ship and subjected to certain medical procedures. There was also another type of case that interested everyone, especially Phil. These cases involved no UFO sighting, and in some of the occurrences the typical gray beings with large heads and slanted or round eyes were not present. Instead, a variety of other beings were reported, including human-like tall blondes, Egyptian-looking humanoids, and religious figures. The fascinating thing about these reports was that the majority of them took place between two and four in the morning.

Using data from the UFOCAT (Unidentified Flying Object Catalog), it was discovered that the majority of UFO sightings seem to peak between the hours of 8:00 and 10:00 P.M., while cases of "High Strangeness" occur between the hours of 2:00 and 4:00 A.M. High Strangeness cases are those that involve the appearance of humanoid or other types of creatures, plus other unusual features including strange sounds, electromagnetic effects, and psychological-physical effects on humans. Physical effects usually take the form of burns, marks on the body, headaches, irritated eyes, and sometimes frequent nose bleeds. Psychological effects consist of changes in the way the person thinks and acts.

Since it was getting late, we were unable to discuss the majority of these case studies. However, we came to the conclusion that the experience of waking up in the wee hours of the morning to find a human or humanoid creature standing by your bed bordered on a psychic experience. In some of these cases the beings floated through the air, appeared out of nowhere, and disappeared into thin air. There were even some cases in which the beings walked through the wall of the person's bedroom as if they were ghosts. In many of these encounters, the person was half-scared to death; in other cases, people lost consciousness, then woke up the next morning with strange thoughts that seem to have been implanted in their minds.

In a small percentage of the approximately 104 cases we studied, we found that there was some type of communication between the person and the entity. The stories that most interested Phil were those in which a being seemed to enter the room by walking through the walls, then pulled the person out of his or her body. The person (or victim) was then taken through a window or the wall into some type of room far removed from their home. Such cases may indicate that some type of interdimensional travel is occurring. We used the information from the San Antonio meeting to help us research and understand the many cases that presented themselves to us in the years that followed.

The case studies below provide examples of encounters with strange late-night or early-morning visitors.

This first case was brought to our attention by a reporter at the *Reporter Dispatch,* a local newspaper based in

Westchester County, New York. The reporter gave us a call after he was contacted by a woman who had a very unusual experience in her home, early in the morning. The reporter had an interest in the paranormal and thought we might want to hear her story, so he arranged for us to meet the woman.

The Paralyzing Beam

Although we try to use the real names of the witnesses whenever possible, in this case it would be best just to refer to the woman as "Jane." Jane is 35 years old and lives with her husband and two young children in their home in Mamaroneck, New York. When we talked to Jane she was still very upset about her experience. Nothing like it had ever happened before in her entire life. Her story, presented below, was told to the authors on June 23, 1992.

On June 20, at 11:00 P.M., Jane was just getting ready to retire for the night. Her husband was already in bed and the two children were fast asleep. As she walked into the bedroom she looked up through the skylight and saw a bright, star-like object right over the window. Jane thought that this was strange because it was so bright, yet she didn't remember ever seeing a bright star in that position. She then got into bed and soon went to sleep.

Several hours later she was awakened by a strange buzzing sound. She opened her eyes and checked the time; it was 3:35 A.M. As she looked toward the skylight, a beam of light came through and hit the foot of the bed. The beam split into a number of colors that looked like a rainbow. The light then traveled up the bed until it was covering half her body. Although she had a sheet on, she could feel warmth from the light. She tried to move and realized that she was paralyzed; she could move only her head. She looked across at her husband and noticed that he was on his back, a position that he never sleeps in. His eyes and mouth were open as if he were dead, but she was relieved to see he was still breathing. "He looked like he was in a trance," she said.

After about two minutes another beam of light came through the skylight. This time it was white. Inside the light, a figure began to materialize. When the light shut off she saw a very tall man standing at the foot of her bed. She told us, "He was dressed in blue robes and was at least seven feet tall. He had long black hair and his skin looked very pale." The being stood there and stared at Jane, and she could do nothing but lie there, paralyzed. The being then raised his hand and pointed to her. He told her verbally that her husband had not been harmed in any way. The being then said that soon she would receive messages that would help the human race through very hard times that were approaching.

Jane blacked out. When she woke up the next day, she told her husband about the experience. Her husband looked at her, laughed, and told her it must have been a dream.

Since the experience Jane claims to be receiving some type of communication from the same being while she is asleep at night. At the present, the messages consist of teachings and predictions of major events that will affect the human race within the next twenty years. Like most of the people who experience contact of this type no definite dates are set for these major events. We believe Jane's story, since she is not looking for publicity and has nothing to gain by reporting this to us. Jane is one of many credible people who have had an incredible experience. This form of contact seems to serve no purpose, but it is our belief that the true nature of the contact is being hidden from the person, at least for the present time.

Sally's Trip

One of the advantages of being a published author is that you receive a great deal of mail in response to the material that you write. We received several more reports of beings, of the same description as the one that visited Jane, that appeared in Texas, Louisiana, and California. The Texas report was the most detailed and interesting of the three. It also involved a woman in her mid-thirties. Her name is Sally Crestman. Sally awakened at about 3:00 A.M., to find a tall man standing by her bed. She described the man as Egyptian-looking, with long, black hair and very pale skin. Although the room was dark, the being seemed to glow, and Sally could clearly make out his facial features. In her letter she told us, "He was just standing there, looking at me. I was so scared that I could not move. My husband was sleeping right next to me, and this was strange—usually he is a very light sleeper, but no matter what I did, I could not wake him up. He was snoring very loudly, although I never heard him snore before. The stranger continued to look at me. His eyes were very dark; a red area glowed in the middle of his pupils. He then raised his finger, pointed to the ceiling, and just vanished, as if he was being beamed aboard like in *Star Trek*. I was so scared—but for some reason, I could not scream. I just pulled the covers over my head. When I did this I heard a voice inside my head say, 'You will now travel far beyond any place you have ever been before.' I then felt as if I was falling into a hole and sinking, and then I blacked out. The next day when I woke up, I felt very tired. My husband said that I looked pale. I went to the doctor and he said that for some unknown reason I had developed an iron deficiency."

Some nighttime visitations by this unknown intelligence do not take place in the bedroom—they take place outdoors. The following is a synopsis of a very interesting phone call that we received from a middle-aged man who lives in Farmingdale, New York. We feel that the individual had a contact experience with some type of interdimensional entity. The witness' name is on file, but it is not important that his name be used in this book. However, our files are always open to qualified researchers into the paranormal, providing that the information is kept confidential.

The Blast of Heat

"I have been living on and off in Saugerties, New York for the past twenty years. During that time I had witnessed two unusual happenings that I thought you might be interested in. Although the experiences took place in 1989, I feel that they will be of some value to your research.

"I have a cabin on the Esopus River. This very narrow waterway runs from the Ashocan Dam to the Hudson River. I live just above the dam at Saugerties. It is a very secluded, wooded area. I have the only property with a sandy beach and waterfront accessibility. It consists of about two hundred and fifty acres, so I really have no neighbors. This gives you an idea of the isolation. I haven't told anyone of this experience to date. I would also like to mention that my home is in a valley between two high mountains. The distance between the mountains is about three hundred feet. Being a pilot, I have landed my aircraft on the Esopus River many times. Now that you have some idea of the area, I can describe what took place.

"It was about 3:00 A.M., and I was awakened by a humming noise. It sounded as if I was in a generator room. I looked out the window but saw nothing, except a glow of light coming from my other home, which is located on the waterfront. I dressed and went to the water's edge. I looked up the river and saw that the glow was coming from a large ball of light. It slowly ascended to tree height, about one hundred feet or so above the ground. This ball of light was about half the size of my three-room house. It hovered for about ten seconds, then moved upward, beyond my line of sight. It was a rather foggy night, which is why I saw a glow instead of a well-defined light.

"I thought it was exciting, and hoped that I had just witnessed a UFO. After a moment my excitement gave way to common sense. I attributed the incident to some freak light distortion from the nearby highway. As I turned to go back into the house, I noticed some small lights in the trees just a few hundred yards away from the house, down a path in a heavily wooded area. The lights seemed strange—like fireflies in the summer, except that this was late in October, too cold for fireflies. I started to walk toward the lights and realized that there were hundreds of them, all over the ground. They seemed to glow like fire ashes in the fireplace, and they looked like they were dancing in the air and avoiding each other, as if they were alive.

"I started forward for a closer look when I felt heat in the area. It was like entering a heated room. I felt a blast of warm, dry heat that made me feel very relaxed, enough heat to make me sweat. I also realized that the closer I got to the lights, the warmer it got, and the more tired and exhausted I became. I could not explain why I suddenly felt this way. It was as if all the energy was drained out of me. Since I was at the cabin alone, I decided not to stay and investigate any longer. I couldn't fight the feeling of exhaustion. I was not feeling sick, just tired. I also recall that the heat was not simply around me; I also felt heat coming down on me from above. The heat from above was far stronger than the heat I felt close to the ground. I looked up to see what could be causing the heat, but only saw an area about thirty feet across that seemed distorted. I thought it might be some kind of infrared radiating area, but from what source, I could not tell. It seemed as if the heat was appearing out of nowhere. Now I know the law of physics, and one basic law states that energy cannot be destroyed or created out of nothing—it has to be changed or channeled in from somewhere else. Well, wherever this energy was coming from, that location was invisible.

"When I looked up I felt the heat blasting against my face, as if there was a heater up there. It was a very strange experience to feel this but see nothing. For a moment I wanted nothing more than to stand there, soaking up this good feeling. The more I stood there the more relaxed I felt. Then, for no obvious reason, I found myself walking back to the house. I don't even remember starting to walk back. I do remember that while I was walking I felt very good, as if my spirit was elevated to the point of being happy for no apparent reason. When I reached my house I went to bed. Before

I closed my eyes I glanced at the time; it was a few minutes before six. This was strange, because I knew that I could not have been out for more that thirty minutes, yet according to the clock there were two hours or so that I could not account for.

"That night's sleep was the most peaceful that I ever experienced in my life. When I woke up the next morning, I went to the location where I had seen the lights to see if I could find any evidence, but I found nothing. I still felt very good, and I didn't give any further thought as to what had taken place until that evening.

"Once I started thinking about it, the more I thought the more confused I became. It was a silly feeling trying to piece the puzzle together. Also, the more I thought about the incident the less clear it became. I decided to write it down, because it was all fading very quickly. I read an article that you (Phil Imbrogno) wrote in a magazine. When I read it, it was like recalling a dream. Ever since that experience I feel that I am not alone. I feel that there is someone with me all the time. Sometimes I get thoughts in my head and I find myself explaining things, like how I feel when I get thirsty and drink a beer, stupid things like that, but I have no control over it.

"There have been times where a multitude of thoughts would pass through my mind and then fade away. These thoughts don't even seem like my own. Since the incident, I have started to recall other strange things that happened to me in the past, things I had forgotten about. One very important incident occurred on June 14, 1988. I was flying my aircraft from Massachusetts to Long Island, along the Long Island south shoreline. At the Jones Beach Tower, the aircraft engine lost power. I was about 500 feet above ground level, over the water near the shoreline, when this took place. According to experts, I had twenty-six seconds to land or I would crash. As I turned the aircraft I saw what appeared to be a silver light in the sky. I was worried about my situation and knew I could not make all the necessary decisions. Then all of sudden a multitude of ideas flashed in my head, and I made all the control adjustments in a very short time. I knew exactly what to do with every control and I landed perfectly. This was impossible. I could have never done that before. Even an expert, super-experienced pilot would have trouble making all those corrections to an aircraft with no engine power. It seemed that for that moment I had the capability to decipher information quickly."

There is no doubt in our minds that the person above had a contact experience. During the two hours or so of missing time it seems that information was programmed into his mind from some unknown intelligence. The heat that he experienced could have been an energy surge from an inter-dimensional source, rather than from an invisible ship. The firefly effect is interesting. In areas where UFOs are seen, that is, areas of magnetic anomalies, these so called "fireflies" are a common sight. We do not believe they were responsible for the above person's experience, but they could be a by-product of the opening of an dimensional portal—a portal opened by an intelligence to establish a link between it and the witness. This witness, a middle-aged male who is a major corporate figure at a large consulting and purchasing company in New York City, may have had contact experiences as far back as childhood. He recalls a number of childhood occasions when he saw strange figures in his room, but the figures never tried to communicate with him.

From our data it is clear that these nighttime visits are not restricted by gender. Out of fifty-two cases that were selected from our files, there are an almost equal number of men and women. The age of witnesses varies from ten to seventy years, although only one incident involved a seventy-year-old man. That investigation was very lengthy and complex, so we will present only a quick synopsis of the case below.

The Image

The elderly gentleman is a successful corporate executive, now living alone in a remodeled farm house near Bethel, Connecticut. For a number of months he had been awakened in the early morning hours by a presence that he knew he had encountered many times before. The occurrences took place several times a month. They began with a face, like a holographic image, appearing on the wall. The face was usually red, pear-shaped, with long slanted eyes, no chin or ears, and a very small mouth. At that point the man always blacked out and awoke the next day, sometimes with a headache, sometimes feeling fine.

This gentleman, whose real name is Bob (we will not give his last name), has a heart condition. During one of these encounters, just after seeing the face, he fell into a sort of light trance and felt hands all over his body. The hands seemed to move him around and he could not open his eyes. He said, "Oh no, not you guys again. Hey, this time why don't you fix my heart?" At that point he felt a warm sensation all over his body which relaxed him and made him drift into a deep sleep. He woke up the next day with no ill-effects. As a matter of fact, he felt quite well.

He had an appointment with his doctor that day and decided to mention the strange things that were happening to him at night. His doctor didn't respond at all to his story except to tell him to come back in a couple of days for another examination. Bob then received a call saying that his next appointment would be at the medical section of Yale University, where a number of experts would review his case.

Bob went to New Haven Yale Medical Center to meet his doctor. She took him into a room where a number of people (all doctors, he assumed) sat in chairs arranged in a semi circle. He sat down, and they began asking him questions about his nighttime encounters with the beings. After about an hour he was escorted out by his doctor. He asked his doctor, "Why all the questions?" She explained that they were all experts in various fields of science, interested in his case. She wanted a number of opinions to make sure that his medication was not having some strange, adverse effect on him. Bob went home more puzzled than before by the events that had become part of his life.

A number of other paranormal activities took place in his home, beginning after the face of the being started to appear. These included the appearance of ghost-like figures in the house, witnessed by a number of people; poltergeist activity in the form of moving chairs and other objects; and strange sounds. Strange burned and brown marks appeared on his lawn in the weeks and months that followed. A brief investigation into Bob's past indicates that he also had a number of paranormal occurrences as a young man, including UFO sightings. His daughter may also have had experiences similar to those of her father, but she would not talk about them to us.

We visited Bob at his home several times and not only witnessed the brown spots on his lawn, but on one occasion also heard a strange humming noise in the house. Phil tried to track down the source of the noise for at least an hour, but it seemed to come from every section of the house. Phil could find no electrical or mechanical cause for the strange sound. The sound was like that of an electric current resonating through fine quartz crystal. The unusual thing was that although it was audible to us, the sound would not record on our tape cassette.

We suspected that the sound was some kind of energy surge—but was it the kind that could cause a dimensional portal to open and allow the beings to enter our universe? Our next step would have been to set up an electromagnetic detector, wired through a chart recorder and an oscilloscope, to record and analyze the frequency and origin of the noise. However, before we could set up the instruments the sound stopped and was never heard again. After the sound stopped, Bob never saw the faces again as far as we know, and to this day the beings, whoever they were, have left him alone.

It was difficult to select the case studies to be used in this book, since so many of them are very interesting. We did not want to leave out any important data that might shed some light on this phenomenon, or perhaps be of importance to the reader. However, we knew that we wanted to include the following incident, one of the most bizarre cases that ever came to our attention. It involved a forty-year-old geologist who was interested in the UFO phenomenon but had never had a close encounter. Although the entire incident could be discounted as a dream, the experience had such an impact on him that it changed his life forever. He told us the story below in May, 1995. At first we were not going to use his contact encounter in this book, because he described it to us in confidence. We now feel that it is much too important to omit. Elements in the story fit with many things that Dr. Hynek told Phil back in 1984.

I Come in Peace

"In was late April. I decided to go to bed; for some reason I was feeling very tired. I mean, I wasn't just tired from the day—I was exhausted, as if I had just taken a sleeping pill. I went to bed and fell asleep in a matter of minutes. I woke up with a jump and heard a buzzing in the room. I looked at the clock; it was 2:45 A.M. I tried to figure out where this sound was coming from. Without warning, the wall on the north side of the bedroom started to glow with a very faint, dull yellow color. I sat up in bed. I really didn't know what the hell was going on. Then this being walks right through the wall, like the wall was a liquid or something. This really shocked me. I saw that he looked like one of the grays that are common in the UFO books I read.

"He was about five feet tall or so and white, not gray. He had a large head and round, black eyes. He was in a black, skin-tight diving suit, and his arms were longer than you would expect for someone that size. I could not see his fingers. He had no ears, and I could barely see his mouth; his lips were very thin. He walked over to the bed and started talking to me, I did not hear him audibly, I heard it inside my head. I have to clarify this: I did not hear a voice, these thoughts were just put into my head. I knew what he was saying and I knew what he wanted.

"He said, 'Don't be afraid, I come in peace. I want to show you something that you have to learn, because we know that in the future you will be in a position to help us.' Now, this was a little strange; I felt no fear at all. This being just radiated peace and good-will. I felt very easy with him—at least, I think it was a him. I got out of bed and followed him, and we went right through the wall. I

Plate 10. Another type of being reported in the 1980–1990 period. This being is similar to the "grays," except the skin tone is like white clay, and the facial features are somewhat different (Composite drawing by Ann Direnger).

found myself in a small room, very dark, that looked like an elevator. He told me that we were in a vehicle that was able to travel through space and time. We were in this room for...well, I really don't know how long we were there. I had no sense of time. There was no sense of motion or anything like that, no noise, nothing. It must have been a short time since I can't remember any conversations with the being at that point. I did ask him his name, and he replied 'Names are not used. We all know who we are by telepathic signatures in our thoughts.'

"Then all of a sudden we were in this lighted corridor. Although I looked up for lights, I didn't see any, yet the entire room was lit in a whitish light that looked a great deal like the florescent lights in a hospital. The being stopped and then, suddenly, we were in a very large room with tables. I looked toward the far end of the room and saw a man and a woman on a table. Now this is the strange part: I knew who they were. Now, when I think about it, I can't remember where I knew them from, but while I was there and saw them lying on the table I even knew their names. They were lying head to head. The woman, who had long black hair, turned her head and smiled at me and said, 'Hi, we are fine.' I asked the being why they were here and he said, 'They volunteered to help us. We have many people who are helping us.' I asked the being where he was from, and he told me that he was from another star system. They have the ability to travel in the closer dimensional windows to our planet. I saw a number of tall men working near tables. They were wearing lab coats and, from the back, they looked human. The being said he had to leave, and one of these human-like beings came over and greeted me. He talked to me; I could hear his voice, and he spoke in English. He had black hair and very round, dark eyes. He looked human to me, but not quite. He told me that he was a hybrid between the human race and the beings; he called them the "travelers." I asked him if he had a name, and he said, 'No, we have signatures in our brains.' He told me that he was a scientist, trained and educated in our medical schools and by the travelers. He told me that there are many like him on the planet, some closer to being human, some more like the travelers.

"The other doctors in the room did not pay attention to me. They seemed quite involved with the work they were doing. I could not see what they were working on at the tables; I was too far away. I did see something move, so I know whatever they were involved with was alive. The hybrid man who talked to me spoke in an unemotional voice, and his face was always straight, like a poker face. He spoke in a monotone; I got the feeling that he was dead serious about what he was saying.

"I then asked him to show me what they were working on. He took me over to a table that looked like it was made of shiny stainless steel. The table had a number of instruments that looked like medical monitors with digital readouts. As I walked closer I was shocked to see a hybrid baby on the table with a number of tubes attached to him. I say 'him' because I could see that he was a male. The child must have been no more than one month old, but he wasn't quite human. I mean, he had human features, but he also looked like the being that brought me here. The skin was more of a dark clay color, and the head and eyes were very large. He was covered in some type of clear, skin-like membrane. The child did not look happy, or healthy.

"The man with me then said that the baby was part of the new generation of hybrid beings. Some type of virus seemed to be killing them, and there was nothing they could do to stop it. He also told me that the travelers themselves are now reduced in numbers. They are desperately trying to survive, but the future looks grim. They were hoping to create a hybrid being who could live in our society—they were in danger of extinction, and this was the only way that they could continue their species, but their plan was not working. He told me that there were other powerful forces in the universe determined to kill off the travelers and all their offspring. He also told me that a secret group in our government was at work, trying to capture the technology offered by the travelers, but since the travelers would not cooperate, this group was trying to wipe them out and steal whatever they could.

"Then, all of a sudden, the being who brought me was standing by my side. He told me that it was time to leave. He said that I would not remember all I was shown, and that this was for their protection. He also said that it would all come back when they called upon me again to help them. He brought me back into the elevator room, and then I found myself back in bed. I woke up the next morning with tears in my eyes. I looked at the clock; it was eight in the morning. I was very tired and also had a very bad headache. Was it a dream? If it was, it was very real. As the day went on I started to forget what took place, like it was disappearing from my mind. I decided to write down everything I could remember while I still could."

This is an incredible story, but we have to consider the possibility that it is true. We heard many stories in which human beings (or near-human beings) were part of contact and abduction experiences. Author Whitley Strieber claims that he was taken on at least one abduction by the gray beings and shown how it was done. Although many UFO researchers doubt Mr. Strieber's claims, we feel that there is a great deal of truth in what he says. There is no question in our minds that he has had numerous contact experiences. Later, many aspects of the story presented above provided a piece of the puzzle that helped explain the mysterious events that were yet to unfold.

CHAPTER SEVEN ...
WINDOWS TO ANOTHER REALITY

Windows, look for windows." Those words from Dr. Hynek stayed with us for years. Dr. Hynek thought that these windows of time and space opened up from time to time and actually acted as a sort of portal by which UFOs could enter our space and time from the fourth dimension. He also thought that these "windows to a parallel reality" were restricted to certain geographic areas. "They are like doors that open and close," he said. This theory could explain why there were so many reports of UFOs in the Hudson River Valley of New York, an area that has been rich in mysterious folklore for hundreds of years.

Being a scientist, Phil was greatly interested by this idea. We began to look for locations where the windows of Dr. Hynek could exist. The first thing we did was to plot on a map all the UFO sightings and other related paranormal activity that we had investigated over the past fourteen years. We choose to restrict the location of our study to south-central

New York, most of Connecticut, and northern New Jersey. We focused especially on Westchester, Putnam, and Dutchess counties in New York, and Fairfield County in Connecticut. It was from these locations that we received the most reports. They were also close enough to us so that we could investigate the encounters in person.

We found that the UFO sightings fell into two categories. The first were the general sightings—that is, cases in which witnesses saw a UFO at an altitude of 1,000 feet or higher. In other words, just a sighting. The second category consisted of cases of "High Strangeness," those cases involving close encounters, and reports that included paranormal phenomena.

The first map we made showed no distinct pattern. It seemed that the UFO had been reported in the entire tri-state area of Connecticut, New York, and New Jersey. We even received about a dozen reports from southern Massachusetts which seemed to concern an object similar to the one seen everywhere else. One interesting thing we noted on the map was that the center, or focus, of all the UFO activity seemed to be in Putnam County, New York, between the towns of Kent Cliffs, Putnam Valley, and Carmel. The UFO seemed to make its first and last appearance in this area. In many of the well-documented reports we were able to trace the object's flight path back to these towns.

The second map was even more interesting than the first. When the cases of High Strangeness were plotted, they proved to be restricted to one geographic location, the exact center of the UFO activity: Kent Cliffs, New York. On this map the reports appeared in clusters, and extended to the nearby town of Southeast, located south of Kent Cliffs. These clusters of paranormal activity were no more than a quarter-mile in diameter. Furthermore, the locations were not random—they were arranged in straight lines!

The next thing we did was to go out and visit some of these locations and see what we could find. This was not as easy as it sounds. In many cases, we had to survey an entire area. We had to trek through heavy brush, and walk miles into the back country where only hunters and hikers go. This required quite a bit of time. Many of these locations remain unexplored as of the writing of this book. While exploring these areas we used ten-meter amateur radio to help our "away" teams keep in touch with a field base. For some reason we did not understand at the time, we had trouble establishing communication with groups over a mile away. Since we were transmitting with a great deal of power (ten times that used in normal radio communication), there was no reason we should not have been able to maintain radio contact. We got a great deal of static, and strange interference that sounded as if it was being generated by a high frequency coil. Because of this problem we switched our communication equipment to two-meter FM. This seemed to work much better; we got less static, and much greater range. We found that the interference generated strongly on the eight- to twenty-meter band in AM radio, and on upper and lower sidebands. This is typical of artificial and natural radio noise, but it was so strong that it jammed radio communications on that band.

One of the things we discovered was that a strange carved standing stone or a stone chamber stood right in the center of the reported paranormal activity at just about every location. At first we thought that this was a coincidence. However, when these stone structures kept on showing up we realized that whoever built them had placed them at these locations for a reason. We also found that the greatest number of these chambers are in the Putnam Valley, Kent Cliffs area of Putnam County, New York.

Our research on these stone structures and the paranormal activity that surrounds them might be the topic of our next book. For those of you who want to learn more, the June, 1994 issue of *FATE* magazine contains a story by Phil Imbrogno. In his story, Phil details some of his research into these structures and discusses the unusual reports from local residents who have experienced paranormal phenomena in and around them. For the purpose of this book, we include a brief history of these stone chambers below. We believe they are connected not only to the UFO sightings, but to all of the other paranormal phenomena reported in the area.

The Chambers

If you take a drive along the back roads of Putnam County, New York, you are bound to see one of these stone chambers, hiding behind a bush or masked by wild flowers. They were called "colonial root cellars" for many years, yet no one knew for certain who had built them, or what purpose they really served. There are at least one hundred and ten chambers in southern New York. Recently, some researchers have made the connection between the chambers and the ancient Druids. It is now thought by many that the chambers were built by Celtic explorers who came to the northeastern United States over two thousand years ago. The evidence comes in the form of an ancient form of script called Ogham (or

Ogam), which has been found at no fewer than three chamber sites. Ogham is an early form of Gaelic. It was translated at the turn of the century by archaeologists who explored similar stone structures in Ireland. The writing on the chamber walls gave dedication to the Celtic festival of Beltane. At two chamber sites, we found carvings in the rock that showed, without a doubt, the constellation Pleiades. What connection does this constellation have with the ancient Druids? Before we explain this in detail we must clarify one point. Although the Pleiades should be a constellation in their own right, they are not. They are actually part of the constellation Taurus, the Bull. The Pleiades are also called the Seven Sisters. Their shape in the sky is eerie; they resemble a ghostly, glittering little dipper.

The Druids believed that when the Pleiades were directly overhead at midnight, the spirits of the earth were at their strongest, and the distance between their world and ours was at a minimum. This celestial placement of the Seven Sisters takes place only at one time during the year, between October 25 and November 5. The date of the Druid holyday was October 31; today we call it Halloween. The Druids may have actually witnessed paranormal phenomena at this time. Many of their legends, telling of strange lights and mysterious beings, sound very similar to our UFO reports of today.

It is also interesting to note that the only other place to find these stone chambers is where the Celtic influence was strong. In Ireland, the chambers were built on what was considered holy ground. This holy ground was often marked by large walls and standing stones, carved in a cylindrical fashion. In Putnam County, New York, we saw that the standing stones and the chambers were very similar to those in Ireland. A great deal of UFO and paranormal activity in Ireland has been reported around these ancient Druid grounds. Stonehenge, in fact, is one of these mystical sites, and has had its share of UFO reports.

Remarkable occurrences that have been reported on and near these ancient Druid grounds in Britain are crop circles:

Crop Circles

Crop circles have an interesting history of their own. They are mentioned as far back as the fifteenth and sixteenth century and in several Shakespearean plays. Today they appear in central Britain in areas that once were considered scared ground by the Druids. The subject of crop circles became popular in the American press in the late seventies and early eighties. At that time, the patterns were simple circles, but since then they have developed into complex, intricate designs.

The crop circles almost always are formed during the night, usually two to three hours before dawn. They are created very quickly; according to researchers, a crop circle may be completed in between thirty and sixty seconds! In one particular case, an area just outside of Stonehenge was surveyed and no circles where found. Several minutes later, the same area was examined again and two crop circles were visible where none had been found before. Crop circle expert Colin Andrews told us that, on one occasion, they saw a strange ball of light over a field. When they went to examine the area, a crop circle was found. It is interesting to note that the Druids also reported strange balls of light at these locations. They thought that they were spirits or energy forces of

Earth; this was one of the reasons that the ground was considered sacred.

In some rare cases, before the formation of a circle, witnesses reported hearing a rustling sound or seeing a mist. On some occasions, one or more lights were seen hovering close to the ground. One report told of a strange, vortex-like wind that appeared out of nowhere. The witness who experienced this said that, as the wind engulfed him, "it took his breath away." Researchers of the Circles Effect Research Group have postulated a theory that the simple circles could be formed by an energetic breakdown of a standing, electrically charged whirlwind—a plasma vortex. Traditional whirlwinds, such as water spouts and dust devils, are driven by convection currents that heat the air, producing an area of low pressure. This causes air to be sucked into the base of the rising column. A plasma vortex is a column of electrically charged particles that could possibly fall apart at the center, causing a violent burst of air. Although this burst of air may explain the formation of the simple circles, it does not explain the formation of the complex designs.

In the past several years it was suggested that the crop circles are the work of hoaxers. However, no circle has ever been found only partially complete, and no hoaxers have ever been caught in the act. Many of the circles and designs appear on the roadsides of very busy highways and near the homes of farmers, yet no human agent has ever been seen creating a crop circle.

One of the most intriguing aspects of the phenomenon is that, if a circle is formed early in the growing season, the grain is bent and continues to grow in that position. Further research has shown that the actual cell structure of the grain has been changed, as if it had been exposed to a strong magnetic field. The circles that are formed after the growing season remain bent, but in no case is the delicate plant structure broken or damaged.

There seems to be only a six- or seven-week window during which the crop circles appear in central England. Perhaps whoever is making these designs has to wait for a window to open to enter our world. There is no doubt that the crop circles are created by some type of intelligence. The evidence suggests that the circles are some sort of message from this alien intelligence from a parallel reality. This would support the "window" theory proposed by Dr. Hynek, because once again we see that crop circles, like the Hudson Valley UFO and other forms of paranormal phenomena, are periodic in nature.

Research has further shown that areas in which the circles and designs are formed contain some sort of magnetic anomaly. When a watch or camera enters the area, the batteries that run these devices seem to be drained rather quickly. Digital watches start to malfunction, as if exposed to an intense electromagnetic pulse. In some cases even video cameras have been reported to go dead, the tape showing nothing but blank "noise." The reason for this effect has baffled even the most skeptical of scientists; no one can come up with a suitable explanation for why this happens.

At the time of the writing of this book, new crop circles have been found. They are crescent-shaped, and seem to be avoiding the more frequently visited places like Stonehenge. It has also been found that the circles appear mostly in the months of July and October. This corresponds to the time during which there are more UFO reports. It is no coincidence that the greatest number of circles have been formed during the last weeks in October, the time of the high Druid Holy Day.

In 1992, Phil had breakfast with Colin Andrews, and discussed his findings of the stone chambers and the unusual phenomena generated from them. Phil mentioned to Colin that the chambers seemed to mark areas of intense magnetic anomalies, and that there was evidence that they were Druid in origin. Colin looked at Phil and told him that he had found the same connection with the Druids where the crop circles were formed in England. It must also be noted that another chamber researcher, Paul Devereux, who lives in England, found a similar connection with the chambers in Ireland, known to be of Celtic-Druid origin.

The Druids

The chambers in southern New York are actually temples, built by ancient Druids who explored the northeastern corner of North America over twenty centuries ago. The chambers were not placed randomly, but were located over areas of magnetic anomalies. A magnetic anomaly is an increase or decrease in the earth's magnetic field. In some of the chambers we found a magnetic deviation almost 20 times above normal. The chambers mark the anomaly, and almost focus this magnetic energy to one point. When the data is graphed it almost looks like a vortex, with the energy being channeled into some unknown, invisible universe.

For years, UFO investigators have made a connection between areas of magnetic anomalies and UFO sightings, but no one was able to prove it. We believe we have definitely made a connection. Most of our readings were taken with a research-grade magnetometer, a device that measures very slight changes in the Earth's magnetic field. Our data has been examined by a number of scientists who all agree that something is causing and focusing the magnetic energy. They speculate that a sphere made of solid iron, buried at least ten feet beneath the earth, might explain the great deviation in our planet's magnetic field at these locations.

UFOs also seem to be attracted to high-tension power lines. For years, UFO researchers speculated that they might tap into the high voltage that the lines provide. We do not believe that these objects would use something as primitive as an electric current. Recently it has been found that these power lines emit a great deal of electromagnetic energy, sometimes referred to as an electromagnetic Pulse (EMP). This EMP energy might be used like a magnetic anomaly to open a window from our universe to wherever the UFOs come from. The UFOs may use this energy to travel in inter-dimensional space by creating a doorway to another dimension. It is no coincidence that the chambers are located in the center of the UFO activity, since the UFOs may use the energy of the anomaly around the chamber to warp space to get into the fourth dimension. Scientists have proposed a theory that the only way to get into this fourth dimension is to warp or twist space, a right angle to a right angle. This would allow someone or something in the third dimension (the one we live in) to enter the fourth dimension.

We believe that the chambers actually mark these "windows" to another reality, since so many strange encounters have taken place around the stone structures. We offer the experience below, which led to the discovery of one of the oldest chambers in the New York area. This chamber sits near one of the largest magnetic anomalies in New York state, where many strange phenomena have been reported. The case presented below is UFO-related; later, we will present two other cases that may involve some sort of contact with a bizarre array of interdimensional beings.

The Hole In The Hill

This encounter was brought to our attention in 1987. To this day, the events remain unexplained The witnesses were two lawyers and their wives, returning home from New York City after seeing a Broadway show. As they left the train station in their car, the driver decided to take a short-cut through the Croton Falls-Southeast area, located on the border of Putnam and Westchester counties in New York. They turned down a very dark, desolate road called "Reservoir Road." It is about two miles long, with no lights. They had to travel slowly; much of the road at that time was not paved, and there were quite a few holes. Normally the driver would never use the road, but on this day he felt almost compelled to take this route. He later told us, "It was almost as if I was programmed to take the road. I could not steer around it. I didn't want to take it because I had a new car and I knew the road was unpaved, with many holes, but I drove down it anyway."

As they proceeded down Reservoir Road, the car's engine began to sputter, then went dead. Although the lights on the car still worked, the engine would not turn over. The two men were sitting in the front seat and their wives were in the back. They all decided that they would wait for a car to pass, or one of the men would try to walk to a nearby home and phone for help. It was late July and the night was very warm, so they decided to roll down the windows and get some air, because the air conditioner was also not working. The driver's friend (the other lawyer), sitting in the front seat, heard something move in the brush up ahead. He grabbed the flashlight from the glove compartment, got out of the car, and walked to the right side of the road. He thought that the noise was made by deer coming out of the woods, and wanted to see them. As he shined his light into the woods the others called out to him, "What do you see? What's making all that noise? It sounds like a herd of deer." The man just stood there, motionless, and made no sound. Then, without warning, he ran back to the car, jumped in, slammed the door, rolled up the window, and yelled, "Let's get out of here! I think they're from outer space!" The others in the car thought he was kidding and laughed—until three creatures came up from the side of the road in single file. All four witnesses agree that the creatures were shorter than a normal man and had very large heads, with no hair and clay-like skin. They also noticed that their eyes were so huge that they covered most of the upper part of their heads. They had long, slender arms, and all three were dressed in some type of dark, tight-fitting suit.

At that point the witness on the driver's side shined the flashlight at the beings. When the light hit their faces the eyes of the beings glowed a deep red. As if frightened, the beings turned around and ran down the hill, passing through the thick brush as if it wasn't there. They then ran into what the witnesses describe as a "hole in the hill." Without warning, a giant, triangular object with rows of multicolored lights appeared right over the area where the beings vanished. The object was constructed of some kind of very dark material and had one large, amber light underneath. The witnesses said that this object was at least 100 feet long from end to end, and was no more than several hundred feet above the ground. The UFO made no noise. It slowly drifted toward their car, all the while projecting a beam of light to the ground which finally engulfed their car. The light was so bright that it blinded the witnesses. They all indicated that they felt a tingling sensation up and down their backs. The light then went off, and when they looked out the car window to see if they could see where the object had gone, they were surprised that it was once again over the same area were they had first seen it. Then, without warning, it vanished as if someone had turned out a light.

As soon as the object was gone the car started up (they had tried it unsuccessfully several times earlier). They sped home and decided not to tell any one about their experience. According to all four of them, the encounter had lasted less than half an hour, yet they arrived home several hours later than they should have.

After hearing this report, the next thing for us to do was to visit the site where the close encounter took place. We found the area with very little trouble and proceeded to explore the brush where the creatures had been seen. The area was very hard to walk through because of thick overgrowth and many thorn bushes. We found it almost unbelievable that a physical being could move through this area with the speed the witnesses observed. They told us that the beings seemed to move through the brush as if it was not there. This led us to consider that the entities may have been only partially physical, and were able to pass through the heavy overgrowth rather than force their way through.

We were intrigued with the report that the beings had seemed to disappear into a hole in the hill, so we slowly and carefully made our way to the area where the beings had vanished. At first we saw a small mound, and then we were very surprised to see what appeared to be an opening in the hill. This opening looked like a small hole and was just barely visible; the thick thorn bushes almost hid it from view. We started to clear out the brush and were quite surprised to discover that the hole in the hill was another one of the stone chambers. This chamber was the smallest that we had found so far and seemed to be crudely constructed. It was partially collapsed, and there were signs that the rock had been weathering for a very long time. This chamber turned out to be one of the oldest ever found in Putnam County. Once again we had made the connection between the location of these chambers, a magnetic anomaly, and the UFO phenomenon.

In 1992, we again heard from the main witness, who had been the driver of the car. He is a well-known attorney in New York City. He told us that all four of them had had several sightings since their first encounter, as well as dreams about the beings. When we asked him about the dreams he replied, "Well, they come into my bedroom, take me and my wife, put us on a table, and then let us go. That's about it." Since that night on Reservoir Road they have lost contact with the other couple, and we have had no success in tracking them down, so we cannot confirm if they are also having the same experiences.

Phil has published a number of stories about these chambers and their connection to the paranormal. This has caused people from all over the country to visit them, and many have had unusual experiences of their own. Some who have taken photographs of the chambers and the area around them have had strange balls of light and glows appear on their film. In one case, a resident of North Salem, New York, claimed that she photographed ghost-like, hooded figures in front of one of the standing stones. This report was never confirmed (we did not see the photograph), but the photographer seemed sincere when she made her report to us. In most cases, these apparitions were not visually seen, yet they showed up on film. Over the years we have collected quite a few reports of paranormal activity, which seems to peak at certain months. The two months with the highest rate of activity are once again July and October. We will explore in greater detail later why this is so. For now, we will point out that the Druid High Holy Day takes places in October, and it is in the last week of October that much of the UFO and other forms of paranormal phenomena have been reported, especially in the Kent Cliffs area.

One strange report of a paranormal occurrence and possible contact case that took place in a chamber located on Route 301 is presented below. This case provides strong evidence that these stone structures mark a bridge to the fourth dimension.

The chamber has had a long history as a site of paranormal phenomena, from UFOs to invisible forces. This chamber is oval, with a double capstone and high ceiling. It is composed mostly of granite, with fine quartz crystals, quartz, and quartzite. Some shale is present near the inside

Plate 11. One of the mysterious stone chambers that sits dead center in an area of high paranormal activity. This chamber is located in Kent Cliff, New York. It is thought that these structures were temples built by Celtic-Druid explorers who came to northeastern North America over 2,000 years ago.

ceiling. This softer material seems to have been used for the inscription of symbols and other forms of writing that might at one time have indicated what the chamber was used for. Today, however, these inscriptions are so weathered that most are indecipherable.

Although there is a magnetic anomaly at this site, it was much lower than those found at other chambers in the area. We suspect that the reading might change from time to time, and increase when a paranormal event is about to take place. We base this theory on the fact that we were able to record an electromagnetic pulse of considerable strength at this location. Several days after that pulse was received on our equipment, the area within two miles of the chamber witnessed a number of UFO sightings. Although there are quite a few people who have had experiences in and around this chamber, we have chosen the story of a local resident of Kent Cliffs, who we will call "Carl." Carl's story is presented below in his own words, as he told it to Phil in the fall of 1992.

Carl's Story

"I was walking down 301 during the late part of the summer of this year (1992), when I passed by the stone chamber on the road. I knew these things have been there for a long time and heard many stories about them. Some think they were built by Vikings or Druids, while others think they were built by the Indians or colonial farmers. To tell you the truth, I never thought much about them and at the time really didn't care. Well, if you're walking at night these things look real spooky, and I know many people who won't even walk in front of them when it is dark. Any way, it was about 11:00 P.M. and it was very dark. The sky was clear, and there was no moon. I walked by the chamber on the opposite side of the road and noticed a faint red glow coming from the inside. This glow was so faint that I could barely see it with my eyes. I also heard a faint sound that was like a hum, sort of like an electrical generator was being used inside to produce electricity to make the light. So I crossed the street and entered what was then (before the road was widened) a short section of woods and entered the chamber. As soon as I walked in the noise stopped and I could not see the red, it was all dark inside. I looked around and felt very uneasy, like someone or something was watching me. You know the feeling, like you're in a dark cellar with someone and you can't see them, but you know someone is there and you are not alone.

"I wasn't in there for more than thirty seconds when this force hits me. It was as if someone pushed me. I fell to the ground, expecting to see someone standing there, but I saw no one at all! As I laid there I felt a presence, like there was someone standing there with me. I slowly got up to my feet and was struck again, this time in the face. It felt like a hand. There was some unseen force striking me every time I tried to get up, so I decide to stay down and not move. I looked toward the opening and saw this figure of a man standing there. He was wearing a white robe and had long black hair and a beard. His hair was very curly and hung over his shoulders. The thing that really scared me almost to death was when I looked into his eyes. His eyes seemed very dark, but they also glowed. The center of his pupils looked red. He just stood there looking at me. When my eyes met his I could feel a tingling up and down my spine. He raised his hand and pointed his finger to me. I got the message that I was not welcome and should leave and never return. Although it was dark I could see him plainly. I don't understand this, but it seemed that he was surrounded by a soft, white glow. The figure dissolved into a cloud of mist, and the mist was drawn into a nearby rock, just as if there was a vacuum there. The entire incident lasted about a minute or two. Then I got up and ran out the entrance, and I never went back. Sometimes at night I wake up in a cold sweat with my heart pounding, because I can still see the image of this guy's eyes starring at me. I always feel that he is waiting for me somewhere in the dark, ready to take me to another place as some kind of prisoner."

Beings of this type have been reported in several of the other chambers close to that area. Sometimes the entity in the white robe is accompanied by several Viking-looking figures, sometimes they are seen with small dwarfs in hooded robes. Are they ghosts, Ultraterrestrials, or aliens? Sometimes the reports also include the strange gray beings that are often reported in UFO abduction cases, as well as the alien reptilian creatures.

The reports are too numerous to dismiss and are made by people who would rather forget that the entire experience took place. Recently, we heard of a new case that occurred around a standing megalithic stone, located on the campus of the State University of New York at Purchase. The witness claims that one night, while he was standing close to the stone, several hooded entities appeared out of nowhere and surrounded him, then vanished after circling him for several minutes. He told us that he could not see their faces, and their hands were covered in the robes. They were no more than four feet tall, and by the way they moved he got the impression that they were more animal-like than human. As they circled him he could hear a faint chant coming from all of them. He did not understand the words, but he compared the sounds to a growl.

The chambers have a definite connection with the UFO sightings in the area. We think they are markers that point to the direction of windows to another reality. When the UFOs appeared in the area they took a definite path. They proceeded to the north, always looped around to the east (toward Connecticut), then finally headed west, to vanish in the Putnam Valley, Kent Cliffs area of New York.

Lake Encounters

When the UFOs were seen in Putnam County, they were often reported hovering around local bodies of water, which are very numerous in that area. These bodies of water are mostly reservoirs that supply New York city with water. Some of them, however, are natural lakes produced in the last glacial ice age, almost eighteen thousand years ago. We were very interested in these lake sightings, since we knew from our past research that at least some of the lakes were fairly strong areas of magnetic anomalies. We had thousands of UFO reports to choose from, so it was an easy task to pick out those cases that took place near or above a body of water. We selected 452 cases, broken down into three categories.

Sightings above the water
    (1,000 feet or more)   276 cases

Sightings at low altitude, near the water
    (between 100 and 200 feet)   83 cases

Sightings at very low altitude
    (less than 50 feet, and at water level)   93 cases

We decided to focus on those reports in which the UFO was fifty feet or less above the water. In many of the ninety-three cases selected, there seemed to be some type of interaction between the UFO and the water. Also, in all of the cases the UFO was reported to be triangular in shape and 100 feet or less in size. We present three typical cases below.

A Reservoir Encounter

The witness, John Falk, has a background in engineering. He had never before witnessed a UFO, or experienced any type of paranormal phenomenon. On March 19, 1983, he was driving home from work on Route 100, passing by the New Croton Falls Reservoir, located near Yorktown, New York in Westchester County. It was two in the morning and the road was quite desolate. He noticed a dark mass sitting above the water and not moving. At first he didn't think too much of it. He was returning home from work and was very tired. Then he began to think that this was quite unusual. He pulled his car over to the side of the road and turned his lights off. He sat in his car for several minutes and watched the object as it hovered no more than fifteen feet above the water in total silence. The object was much darker than the light-polluted background, so he was able to see that it was triangular in shape and very large. He was about 500 to 700 feet from the UFO at this point, parked near Muscoot Farm Park, a very dark section of the road.

After several minutes the object started to move. A row of red lights appeared up and down the chevron of the triangle. He told us that the color of the lights was very similar to that of a helium-neon laser; he was amazed at the purity of the red. The object then began moving very slowly around the water. He rolled down his window and was amazed that an object of that size could move so slowly and make no sound. He thought that it might be some type of government experimental craft doing research in the area, but then thought that this was impossible. He was sure that this thing was not of this earth. How he knew this he doesn't know. He told us, "It was just the feeling I had when I watched it move and saw those lights. I knew it was not of human design." He got out of his car, walked through a wooded area, and stood at the edge of the reservoir. The object started slowly drifting toward him. The UFO was now no more than 200 feet from him. He noticed that it was made up of some kind of gray material that was very dark. The object seemed very smooth, and he could not see any joints or sections. Except for the red lights, most of the object was dark, but he could also see a faint red glow that seemed to come from the underside of the UFO and reflect off the water.

As he continued to watch the UFO he noticed a car approaching the reservoir area. As the car's headlights came closer, the lights on the UFO went out. All that was visible was a dark mass, which would have been barely noticed from the road. As the car passed the lights on the object went back on, and the UFO continued its sweeping motion over the water. This took place three more times during Falk's twenty-minute sighting.

The object came to within 100 feet of him, and then stopped. The UFO then began moving to his left with very slow, circular motions. He still noticed the red glow from the bottom of what he called "a massive ship." Then, without warning, the object projected a thin, red beam of light that, according to Falk, looked like a laser beam. This laser came from under the object and shot into the water below. The object then shut off the beam, moved to another location, and the beam came on once again.

The UFO did this for several minutes. Then it quickly moved back to the center of the reservoir. The object hovered above the center of the body of water for about fifteen seconds, and all the lights went out. The object then emitted a blinding burst of white light that seemed to be directed at Falk, knocking him to the ground. The next thing he remembered was getting up from the ground. It was no longer dark; it was daylight. When he looked at his watch he saw that it was just after eight in the morning. Falk is sure that the entire sighting was only twenty minutes or so long, yet he lost consciousness for several hours after being hit by the light beam from the UFO. His wife told us that during the next couple of days her husband seemed out of reach and disoriented.

Another Reservoir Encounter

The Falk encounter is very similar to another case that Phil and Dr. Hynek investigated back in 1983. That case also involved a person with an engineering background, and the location of the sighting was at the Croton Falls Reservoir in Mahopac, New York. The encounter also took place in the early hours of the morning. The witness to the event was Jim Cooke, a biomedical engineer in his early forties who designs equipment for laser optics and laser surgery. He was driving to his home in Mahopac, New York from nearby Croton Falls on October 28, 1983, at about 2:30 A.M.

"I was driving up Croton Falls Road from Route 6. As I went around a bend, I noticed these lights in the trees. They looked like the lights of an aircraft, so I didn't think much about it. I continued along the road, with the Croton Falls Reservoir on my left. The lights approached very fast from off in the distance until they were very close to the reservoir. They dropped down much too quickly to be a plane. The object just hovered above the trees, and I slowed down to get a better look. All I noticed at this time was that the lights were off. All I could see was this huge dark mass behind the trees. It looked like no aircraft that I ever saw in my life."

Cooke stopped his car and got out, but the trees blocked his view. He stood for two or three minutes watching through the trees and finally got up enough nerve to try for a closer look.

"I started to walk through the trees to the shoreline. I got to the shoreline, and I could see this object just hovering no more than fifteen feet above the water. It was still dark, but I could see it was triangular in shape. It had a highly nonreflective surface. I could see the dark mass, but I couldn't make out any detail at all. I did airplane repair work for four years in the service and this material was like none I had ever seen before. This object was about 200 feet from me and I could hear no sound. Then some red lights came on, on the sides of the triangle; they looked like the red LED lights on digital display devices. Then something came from the underside of the object, a red beam of light or something solid that was glowing red, I really don't know what, but it seemed to be probing the water. As I continued to watch the object, it moved to four different locations over the reservoir. Each time it would stop and project the red beam probe into the water. The object maintained a steady altitude of about fifteen feet.

"I noticed that, several times, when the object projected this probe, a screen came down to the water. It seemed like this probe was behind the screen, or in it. If you ever looked through infrared waves, you can see the background distorted behind them. This is what it looked like—a heat screen. As I watched the object drop this probe into the water, the probe would glow, and then the curtain or heat screen or whatever it was would appear. The curtain would then vanish when the probe retracted and the object moved to another part of the reservoir.

"My first impression was that the probe was a solid light source, because it seemed to have the same density throughout its width and length. The color of the probe was cherry red; it looked like it was very hot. Several cars passed at this time, and each time a car got close the lights on the object went out and the object became motionless. There were times when the lights went out that this thing was just about invisible, and even from my vantage point I could barely make out its outline.

"I really don't know how long I watched the object. I was so amazed that I lost all track of time. After it finished probing the water it just lifted up at a thirty-five degree angle and was lost in the sky. As for its size, I would have to say that it was at least 100 feet long and thirty feet at its base. I don't know what it was. I still wonder what it could have been and why it was fooling around with the water."

The next lake encounter case that we will present took place over Putnam Lake in Brewster, New York. The witnesses were both young women in their early thirties. Once again, the sighting took place at night. What follows is the sighting account, as told to us by one of the witnesses, Sue Hanson, a resident of the Patterson, New York area.

Sue's Story

"Kris and I were returning home from work. We often car-pool to save gas, since we live only several miles from each other in the Brewster-Patterson area. On July 12, 1987 we were driving down Fairfield Drive. Off to the right was Put-nam Lake. Just above the lake was a bright circle of lights that were all white in color. The circle was high above the lake, just sitting there in the sky. I called out to Kris and said, "Look at that!" She said that it was probably a blimp. I said that there was no way this was a blimp; I'd seen blimps in the area before, and this looked nothing like them. I slowed down and watched the lights come down from the sky toward the north end of the lake. I pulled down Lake Shore Drive and drove to the side of the lake, where I could get a better look at the lights. The time at this point was about 11:30 P.M. We got out of the car and walked to the shoreline, which was only about fifty feet from the road. This is a pretty lonely place and we were a little scared to get out of the car.

"The UFO, and I say UFO because we did not know what it was, then moved across the water no more than twenty feet above the lake. There seemed to be some sort of heat screen or shield extending down into the water, coming out from under the object. The object then projected a beam of light into the water, the lights began vibrating, and I heard a buzzing sound. I could now make out a sort of shape—the UFO was triangular, like a pyramid. The UFO vibrated faster, and the buzzing got louder and louder, so loud that we had to hold our ears. Then, without warning, the lights on the object went out and the object just vanished. We got very excited, because we knew that we had just seen a real UFO, so we got in the car and drove to the state police on Route 22 in Brewster. We told the officer on duty what we had seen, but he looked at us and said, "UFOs are not our jurisdiction. You have to call NASA or the Air Force." He even asked us if we had been drinking. I was very insulted. Then he said, "Oh, you must have seen those guys flying ultralight aircraft out of Stormville Airport. They always try to fake a UFO," and he laughed. I felt very foolish and angry. We left, and decided not to tell anyone else about the sighting."

In all ninety-three cases, the objects chose artificial lakes and reservoirs. There were no low-altitude body-of-water encounters over natural lakes. We considered this information quite interesting. A pattern was now emerging. We knew from past research that UFOs are attracted to bodies of water, especially lakes and reservoirs. In all of the lakes we investigated we found a compass deviation of between .32 and 2 degrees, showing the presence of a magnetic anomaly. But why did the UFO only pick man-made bodies of water? Part of the answer may be the fact that some of the natural lakes that were investigated showed only a .10-degree deviation in the compass. The readings at artificial lakes showed anomalies as much as twenty times stronger!

The reason for stronger anomalies in the artificial bodies of water is clear. The geological composition of most of the area includes iron ore. Natural lakes were formed during the last ice age, when glaciers carved out the rock below to create basins, which later filled with water to form the lakes. The glaciers, however, did not expose all of the iron ore. A thick layer of granite remains on top, covering the iron. The artificial lakes and reservoirs were made during the twentieth century, with the help of machinery and blasting. They are much deeper than the natural lakes. The iron ore is totally exposed, which explains why the magnetic anomalies are stronger over these areas. Residents here have always complained about too much iron in their drinking water; water filters clogged frequently. For years, researchers have been trying to make a solid connection between these anomalies and UFOs. I believe that we are the first to do so.

As we sat and discussed our findings, we wondered if whoever was behind the UFOs was responsible for opening up these four-dimensional windows in the magnetic anomaly areas. Are conditions better at certain times for windows to open? Do the intelligences need the UFOs to open and close them, or do they open up naturally on a regular basis?

Our findings indicate that there are times when UFO sightings and paranormal phenomena are more frequent. We began to look for a correlation between an event and the UFO reports. We decided to look into the matter of the phase of the moon. Is there a connection between the lunar cycle and UFO sightings? Some researchers seem to think so; we had received several calls in the past from well-known UFO investigators who insisted that the majority of sightings take place at the new and full moons.

The idea that the phase of the moon has something to do with the appearance of UFOs captured our interest greatly. The moon's gravitational influence on the earth is very strong. We can see this effect on the oceans of our planet. Perhaps the moon triggered something that opened these windows into the fourth dimension. We began looking through the hundreds of reports that we had received over the past several years and noting the lunar phase at the time of each sighting. A result of our study is shown in graph form in chapter 13. Using a computer, we matched 876 cases (for which the time and date was accurately known) with the phase of the moon. We were very surprised to find a peak of sightings three days after the full moon, and three to four days after the new moon. It was clear from our study that there was, in fact, a definite connection between the phase of the moon and the appearance of UFOs.

The evidence was overwhelming. Sightings did not increase during the new and full moons, but several days after. It seems that it took several days for the gravitational influence of the moon to trigger an opening in the windows into this parallel reality. Many of the encounters that took place after the full or new moons were quite dramatic. Most were close encounters, in which some type of contact was established with the witnesses.

One such experience took place near the Rocky Mountains on November 29, 1993. It was late at night, just before the start of a lunar eclipse. The witnesses, a 37-year-old truck driver named Tom Mullin, and his 30-year-old girlfriend were on the west side of the Rockies, heading back to New York State. Below is Tom's description of what took place that night, as told to us several weeks after the encounter.

Transported Through The Rockies

"We were heading back to New York from a vacation in California. It was November 29, at about 11:00 P.M., and we were in Colorado, about thirty miles from the entrance to the mountains. It was a very clear night, a little chilly, and there was a full moon. It was the night of the lunar eclipse, so I wanted to get up into the mountains before the eclipse took place so that we could get a better look at it.

"We were driving on a flat, straight road when I looked up and saw a bright red, star-like light that was slowly moving across the sky. I thought at first it was a satellite, but then it stopped and shot straight down below the horizon. I thought that this was strange and wondered what it was, since no satellite or aircraft can do what I saw this light do. About five minutes passed; then another ball of light shot up from the horizon, and then slowly moved overhead. As it reached a point directly above the car it seemed to move at the same speed that we were moving, so it appeared motionless. It was a red ball of light. It was impossible to tell how high it was, maybe 2,000 feet or so. I tried speeding up and slowing down, but the object stayed directly over the car. My girlfriend said that it looked like it was spying on us, checking us out. This was real freaky, because there was no one else on the road with us. The thing followed us for another ten miles, then just streaked backward, and I lost sight of it. We continued to drive, and I put on the radio and listened to some station on the west side of the Rockies.

"A short time later I started to get static on the radio. I thought that the mountains were blocking the signal. Then I looked out the rearview mirror and saw a light in the distance, on the road, approaching very fast. It was getting brighter and brighter and then all of a sudden—FLASH—it was right behind us, about ten feet off the ground. It looked like some kind of disk and was red and white, white toward the center and red around the edges. The object was about three times the size of the car and moved with no sound. It was a sort of fluorescent white and red. I could see no windows.

"I stepped on the gas. We were moving 90 miles an hour, but the ship kept right up with us with no effort at all. It was only about ten feet behind my car—it did not matter if I sped up or slowed down, it kept the same distance from us. My girlfriend started screaming that they were aliens and they were going to get us. I started to think that they were going to capture us and take us to some zoo on another planet or something like that.

"As I watched in the rearview mirror, a figure appeared at the very front of the ship. It was strange; it was as if he was always there but could not be seen because of the light. Only when he came very close to the front could I see the outline of the figure clearly. It was very slim and seemed to have a large head with big, slanted eyes. Although his entire body was in a shadow, his eyes were glowing yellow. Then I heard a voice inside my head say, "You will not be harmed. We are interested in studying you and the female." When I heard the voice there was this buzzing sound also. Well, I didn't care who or what they were. If they wanted to communicate with the human race, why pick us? I yelled out, "Get away, I don't know nothing."

"The car was now going very fast. We were approaching the entrance to the Rocky Mountains, the eclipse was just beginning...and then all of a sudden we were on the east side of the Rockies, the eclipse was over, and the moon was setting in the west. I was shocked to see a sign right in front of us that said we were approaching Denver. Somehow we got transported through the Rocky Mountains.

"We continued to drive and hardly talked to each other. We stopped at the nearest motel and took showers; we both felt very dirty and extremely tired. We stayed there that night and left for New York in the morning. Nothing else happened after that."

In this case there seem to be at least four hours of missing time. This is a very unusual abduction case, to say the least, since the car was also taken. The mileage on the car showed only eighteen miles between the time of the close encounter with the UFO and the moment they found themselves on the east side of the Rocky Mountains, although the actual distance is over 150 miles. We also questioned them about the amount of gas in their car, and it seems they still had almost three-fourths of a tank after crossing the mountains.

One of the most obvious things we learned from these cases is that there does seem to be some kind of connection between magnetic anomalies and the phases of the moon. Perhaps the UFOs are looking for a key or sign to tell them when the next window will open to the fourth dimension. All of the information we have obtained tells us only part of the story. Perhaps someday we will be able to put all of the pieces together and come up with an answer we can fully understand.

CHAPTER EIGHT ...

THE ALIEN FACTOR

During July of 1984 a strange, small news editorial appeared in the *New York Post*. The *Post* was a very popular newspaper that served not only the city, but also the suburban area and Connecticut. The editorial was actually a letter, sent by someone who asked that his name not be used, about the UFO sightings that were taking place at the time. The writer wrote about underground bases that were being used by the government in the Brewster, New York area. Although these underground installations are mentioned in *Night Siege,* we never were able to locate the entrances. The area in question is very rural, and we were quite busy at the time investigating the countless close encounters. The article interested us because the writer seemed familiar with the area and was pretty sure of his facts. The text of the editorial appears below:

"Why are people seeing all these UFOs all of a sudden in the Hudson River Valley area? The answer is simple: there seems to be some kind of underground activity in the Brewster area in the old abandoned iron ore mines. Some years ago the government went out of its way to purchase the land that the mines are located on and people who live in the area, including myself, have seen military vehicles entering the dirt roads. They never come out. Also, we have seen helicopters landing in the hills close to the mine entrances. These areas are rich in sightings of UFOs, and people who live close to the mines have reported strange sounds and unusual lights. I feel that the government has established an underground base in which some type of experimental aircraft is being kept. There is also a possibility that the mines are being used by our government and an alien intelligence to hide some type of operation in the area."

(Signed) Anonymous

If this letter printed in the *Post* was not enough to arouse our interest, three years later, in 1986, just before the publication of *Night Siege* Phil received a call from a CIA operative who lives in the southwest. Since Phil had a background in military intelligence he still had limited contact with individuals who were still working in the CIA, and in Army and Air Force intelligence. The caller told Phil that he had come across a number of documents that were actually supply requests for an underground operation in the Brewster, New York area. The documents said that the operation was located in an old iron ore mine near that town, but they failed to mention what mine was used for this underground operation. The informer told Phil that, according to what he found out, the underground base was a lab being jointly used by a special operations unit and an unknown alien intelligence. The purpose of this underground lab was unknown, but the operative told Phil that he saw lists of equipment that might be used in biological experiments. Shortly after this phone call took place, this individual could no longer be reached. It seems that he no longer had an active phone number. None of the mail that was sent to him was returned to us, so it must have been intercepted by someone. To this day, Phil cannot locate the CIA operative who gave him this information.

Our next step was to try to find out what was going on in the old mines and the surrounding area. It wasn't until 1989 that Phil began tracking down the mysterious entrances to see if there was any fact behind the information that had been handed to him years before. During that summer, Phil began looking at areas featured in many reports, not only of government activity, but also of UFO sightings. He decided to take a hike through the woods near the Croton Falls Reservoir in the town of Southeast, New York. This location has been the site of more than its share of paranormal events over the past ten years. The land around the reservoir is sparsely populated; if you were going to hide some type of covert operation, this would be the place to do it.

As Phil looked over the area and walked down some of the back trails, he noticed the tire marks of four-wheel drive vehicles. This did not mean too much, since hunters use the area when certain game is in season. He proceeded down Reservoir Road, then came to another road that was blocked off. The road was labeled on the map as "Upper Magnetic

Mine Road." He got out of his car and saw quite a few "No Trespassing" signs on the trees, posted every thirty feet. He began to walk up the narrow road. Tire marks in the soft dirt seemed to have been made by a jeep. As he went further up the road, he began to see large stones of iron ore scattered around. He knew he was getting close to the mine entrance.

He heard someone behind him and stopped. When he turned around he saw a police officer, running very quickly toward him, and commanding him, "Stop, and go no further." Phil was a little surprised, but stopped. The officer, a member of the Putnam County Sheriff Department, informed him that he was trespassing on land that was owned by the federal government, and that no one was allowed up the road. When he asked the officer, "Why?" the officer said that he did not know; he just had orders to keep people out of that area. The officer escorted Phil back to his car and told Phil to follow him. The officer led Phil to Route 22 and told him to leave the area. If he was caught trespassing again, he would be arrested. Phil left, but he knew he had to come back and find out what was at the top of the hill.

Two weeks later, Phil went back to check out the area. This time, he decided to come in through the back way, Route 22 in Brewster. He parked his car near the side of the road and walked a mile or so into the woods. He tried to estimate his location, and came to a ridge overlooking what seemed to be a driveway, a house, and a number of smaller buildings. As he watched the area he noticed a Jeep come up from the road. It pulled up just outside a house, and two men got out. They were dressed very neatly and had short hair; they looked like police or federal agents. Using binoculars, Phil was able to get a good look at them. In his opinion, they looked like typical military personnel. The men entered the house, which did not seem to have drapes or other things that would indicate a home. It almost looked like a safe house being used by federal agents. It was strange to find a house so deep in the woods with only one route, a dirt road, leading in and out.

Phil also noticed a number of power lines and telephone cables running to the house and the small buildings around it. Someone had gone to a great deal of trouble and expense to maintain this installation. As Phil continued to watch, two large dogs came out of the house and started patrolling the area. They approached the location where Phil was lying down, and started looking in his direction. Although the dogs were too far away for him to tell what breed they were, he thinks they were Doberman Pincers or Rottweilers. Phil became a little nervous; the dogs seemed to know that he was there and began barking. At that point one of the men came out of the house and started looking in the direction where Phil was hiding, using binoculars. Then the man quickly ran back inside. Although the dogs did not advance any further, they continued to bark. Phil decided to leave the area. He carefully and quietly made his way through the woods and back to his car.

Phil left more puzzled than before. Who were these men, and why did the local police go out of their way to make sure that no one traveled up that path? Most important of all, what was up there? We were to find a possible answer to that question later on, but first, a series of events took place that started to lead us in a different direction.

Since the early eighties, there have been all kinds of stories about secret deals made between some unknown alien intelligence and the secret government of the United States. Just who is the secret government? The people who really run this country are not the elected officials, but the heads of the various known and secret intelligence agencies. Elected officials are only in office for a limited amount of time, after which they usually become civilians. This includes the President. The heads of the intelligence organizations, such as the CIA, NSA, NSC, and Naval Intelligence, are in those positions for life. These individuals have considerable power and are in charge of all the covert operations that are not funded through Congress. It is these secret organizations, in fact, that hold most of the UFO files.

Recently, a well-known group that is against UFO secrecy actually sued the CIA and the Air Force to force them to release a number of documents that involve military interaction with the UFO phenomenon. First, the court ruled that the people of the United States have the right to know and the documents should be made available to the public. The lawyer for the CIA then asked the judge to review his decision behind closed doors. Shortly thereafter, the judge reversed his decision, stating that the information in the documents was vital to the security of the United States, and the public does not have the right to see them after all. For years the Air Force has been telling us that the UFO phenomenon does not exist. If there is nothing to these stories, then why are almost 200 documents being withheld? Also, why, in the many hundreds of documents that have been released, has most of the information been blacked out?

As we investigated this matter further, we were told an intriguing story. We don't know whether or not it is true, but our source was very dependable, and we feel it should be considered as fact. The story is a bizarre tale of how the United States government made a deal for technology with an alien race from another dimension. The story is very complex; we relate it to you as it was told to us back in 1991.

It seems that the major governments of our planet know that an alien intelligence from another star system has been exploring the earth for centuries. Although these aliens remained hidden, during the twentieth century the United States government discovered their existence. This information was restricted to the top-secret intelligence organizations, and a great effort was made to keep the information about these visitors from the public, and from the other governments of the world.

This alien intelligence had been involved with genetic experiments on human beings for countless centuries. Some feel that it is their manipulation that has produced modern human beings. Attempts were made to communicate with the aliens, but the aliens refused to meet with the leaders of these covert operations. By the end of World War II, several meetings were arranged with the aliens. One of these meetings took place at a well-secured military base. The entire meeting was filmed. Alien ships landed, and there was an exchange of limited information between our society and the alien culture. The movie *Close Encounters of the Third Kind* is supposed to be an exaggerated reenactment of this meeting with the aliens.

It was found that the aliens are from a nearby star system. It seems that they were having a severe genetic problem and were dying. They needed human beings to infuse fresh DNA into their species, so that their race could continue rather than die out. According to the person who told this story to us, many people walking around today are a hybrid race, a certain percentage of their genetic material alien, the rest human.

The government of the United States wanted technology from the aliens, but they refused to give us anything for which they felt we were not ready. An exchange program began—we allowed the aliens to abduct certain people and perform genetic experiments, in exchange for limited technology. It is rumored that this is what started the boom in microchip technology in the early seventies. However, this covert faction of our government wanted more technology, especially in the area of weapons. When the aliens refused to cooperate, orders were given to capture or shoot down all alien craft in the hopes of stealing the technology, since they would not give it to us.

This story made sense to us. Several years ago, Phil had a conversation with a high-ranking ex-Air Force fighter pilot, who told him that they had standing orders to shoot down all objects reported as UFOs. Although it seemed that the aliens were a non-hostile race, they did what was necessary to defend themselves. We have collected a number of cases in which fighter pilots had their weapons and electrical systems fail while they were in pursuit of a UFO.

A sort of one-sided war began between the secret government and the aliens. The secret government did everything it could to bring down alien craft, but was no match for the alien technology. Then a strange twist of fate occurred that changed the balance of power and created a balance of terror.

Using some of the technology that was given by or captured from the aliens, a secret project began to unfold somewhere around 1948. This project was called "Project

Invisibility," and involved making objects invisible by warping space around them using high frequency generators. The experiment was developed at Princeton University. According to our informant, the first time the device was used it didn't work, because the system required too much power. When the power problem was solved (we don't know what the new source of power was, but there is a rumor that it was something called element 117, which was supposed to have been captured from the aliens) there were some unexpected effects.

Humans were unable to enter the field that was generated because they became disoriented. Electromagnetic radiation was somehow short-circuiting the electrical impulses between the synapses in the brain. In some cases, according to our contact, the result was madness, followed by death. However, when the power of the device was increased, strange lights began to appear in the room. There were even stories of strange images appearing, images of what seemed to be Earth's past. Had they created some sort of bridge between the present and the past? The researchers, however, were unconcerned with the materializing images because the device produced the desired effect. Many things in the test area disappeared and, when the device was turned off, they reappeared in perfect condition. The device worked well with non-living things, but living creatures seemed to suffer greatly. In many cases, when the experiment was performed using something living (often some type of animal), the living creature would vanish and not return.

It is not known why the researchers decided to go ahead and test the device on a Navy ship with a full crew. Perhaps someone thought they had solved the problem they had with living matter. The test was conducted sometime before

1950, on a ship near the Gulf of Mexico. This experiment was wrongly named the *Philadelphia* experiment, and was publicized in a number of books and two movies. However, the material that has been made available to the public consists mostly of misinformation. The ship was not named the *Philadelphia,* and the location was not off the east coast, as one might expect.

The equipment placed in the ship consisted of a number of high-frequency generators, but the power source that activated these devices is unknown. It is suspected that it was nuclear, or something else obtained from the alien technology. A transmitter placed aboard the ship sent out a coded signal so that the ship could be tracked. However, when the ship disappeared the signal also vanished. Several seconds later, the signal was once again received—indicating that the ship was now almost 200 miles east of its previous location.

Naval intelligence hurried to locate the ship, now drifting near the west coast of Florida. When they boarded it they found something very strange. First of all, the electrical equipment on the ship was either not working properly, or destroyed. The ship itself had sustained severe structural damage, as if it had been through a battle. However, the most terrifying discovery concerned the crew. A considerable percentage of the crew was unaccounted for, including the captain. Many of the remaining crew members behaved like raving lunatics. Further medical examination showed that their brains seem to have experienced a short-circuit from some type of sensory overload. Several crew members who survived seemed to be in fairly good shape. These crew members were interrogated by officers of Naval Intelligence, who asked them how all this could have taken place in the few seconds during which they had vanished. The crew members looked puzzled. According to them, they had been gone for weeks (or months; they weren't sure). It seems that a strange dilation of time had taken place. Wherever they had gone, time ran on a different scale.

One of the most amazing things that they talked about was meeting a strange race of beings after the ship vanished. They claimed that they actually went into another universe that was void of sensation or anything else. There were no trees, no water, no sun in the sky. They said that they were in some type of glowing, yellow-white fog that looked like the Christian version of limbo, a place between heaven and hell. In this limbo, a number of strange creatures approached them and came aboard the ship. These beings looked like giant insects, but stood upright and were able to communicate with the crew. The crew members described how they became like laboratory animals. That was why most of the crew was missing, dead, or insane. The beings wanted to know more about us, so they used the crew of the ship for experiments. The strange beings also seemed interested in our world, but didn't seem to have a way to get here. The experiment had allowed us to enter their world; it was like a window that could only be opened from our side. The crew members didn't really know how they finally got back. They just found themselves once again aboard the ship and back in the water.

Naval Intelligence was very interested in the beings in this other dimension. Soon the information spread throughout the intelligence circles of the United States government. The secret government was very interested in learning what technology could be obtained from these beings. The aliens who had been here for a very long time refused to cooperate fully and would not give us weapons of mass destruction.

The devices were used once again. This time the beings came into our world and made secret deals with the government. They were interested in our universe and knew that the window was one-way (at the time); we had to open it from our side in order for them to come through. The beings (who are interdimensional in nature) started to perform their own genetic experiments on humans. Our government allowed these experiments in exchange for technology. The difference between the experiments conducted by the extraterrestrials, and those performed by the interdimensionals, is that the ETs were very gentle and did not hurt anyone, but the interdimensional beings did not care for the safety of their subjects, who were treated more or less like experimental rats in a laboratory.

The interdimensional beings became very concerned about the ETs and wanted them out of the picture. They worked with our government to wage a sort of war on them and slowly began to wipe them out. Our contact told us that the interdimensional beings created a virus (like the AIDS virus) that attacked the ETs and their hybrid offspring. This resulted in over 80% of them becoming sick or dying. The story goes on to say that the ETs (sometimes called the grays) have been just about wiped out, and this new race is now the one being seen and reported as UFOs. The interdimensional beings are often called the insects or reptilians. Disk-shaped UFOs are now rarely seen; they have been replaced by triangular craft. All experimental government craft, including the Stealth Bomber, are now triangular in shape. Our contact feels that stealth technology and other super-secret aircraft were actually obtained from this deal with the interdimensional reptilian beings.

We have no reason to think our contact is lying. We are certainly convinced that he feels he is telling the truth as he knows it. If this story is real, then it seems that the interdimensional beings did not actually achieve a foothold in our universe until the late 1970s. It is at this time that triangular craft started being seen more often than the cigar- or disk-shaped UFOs. The UFO that was seen over the Hudson Valley was triangular in shape, and behaved much differently than the UFOs in past sightings in that area. The triangular craft was more aggressive; it did not avoid being seen. The available evidence indicates that these interdimensional reptilian beings were the intelligence behind this series of sightings.

The government continued contact with these beings right into the 1970s. Although some of this information slowly leaked out to the public, no one took it seriously at the time. UFO investigators often wondered why most of the UFO documents were held by Naval Intelligence and why many UFO sightings were in fact channeled to this organization. The reason was that the Navy was the first to make contact with these interdimensional beings. Later, many more covert operations in the government got involved, as they all rushed to obtain the new technology that was being offered by these interdimensional aliens.

The secret government thought they had the entire situation under control. Then, something happened. The beings had secured a foothold in our world and were now abducting more people than their original deal with the government had specified. As far as we can tell, the deal was that, in exchange for technology and information, the secret government would allow abductions to take place. A list of individuals was to be sent to a government operation that would keep track of the entire situation. When the abductions got out of control, this organization become concerned, and attempts were made to stop the aliens and close the dimensional window between their world and ours.

According to the story we were told, the attempt to shut the window was unsuccessful. Our contact told us, "The invasion is over; all we are waiting for is the screaming." We were told that this is the main reason that the government does not tell people about the UFO situation, and why they have gone out of their way for years to discredit witnesses. How would the people of this country react if they knew that their government allowed an alien intelligence to abduct them and experiment on them in exchange for technological advances?

Much of the information about Project Invisibility comes from an individual who witnessed the entire event. This person is not the same man who gave us the story above, but another individual. He had a conversation with *Night Siege* co-author Dr. J. Allen Hynek about twenty years ago. An intelligence officer for the Navy, this person was there when the entire incident took place. The information that he gave Dr. Hynek verified our contact's story, which is why we seriously consider its validity.

The former intelligence officer met with Dr. Hynek in Mexico and used the alias "Carlos Allende." Allende was the town in Mexico where the first meteorite that contained organic molecules was recovered. The discovery of organic molecules in a meteorite proved that the building blocks of life are common in space, strong evidence for the possibility of extraterrestrial life forms.

Carlos met with Dr. Hynek and told him a shorter version of the story of the interdimensional beings and their deal with the secret government. When Dr. Hynek came back from Mexico he told Phil, "Carlos Allende is a real person. I met him in Mexico—he's sort of a vagabond, wandering around that country. He is very paranoid that he is on our government's hit list. I loaned him some money for food and he went on his way." In 1980, while Phil was attending class at M.I.T. in Boston, a long-distance telephone call came to his home in Connecticut. When he arrived home several weeks later he was told that he had received a collect call from someone called Carlos. Since he wasn't there, the call was not accepted. Phil wonders to this day if the caller was the mysterious Carlos Allende. Carlos was one of the lucky ones who did get away. It is rumored that many people who were involved with Project Invisibility mysteriously died or vanished.

We don't know if the information we have gathered is the absolute truth, but there is evidence to indicate that it should be taken into consideration by serious UFO researchers. The story closes by saying that the aliens were able to take over or establish a number of underground bases. According to our contact in the CIA (as mentioned at the beginning of this chapter) at least two such bases were located right in our backyard, that is, in Putnam, Orange, and Ulster Counties of New York. We knew the general location of the underground entrances, and we heard many stories of strange phenomena around these locations. It wasn't until 1995 that we actually found the entrances. Chapter Nine presents the results of our explorations into these underground areas.

CHAPTER NINE …

UNDERGROUND

It is not unusual to hear rumors of unexplained experiences surrounding the old mines of the greater New York area. Reservoir Road, in the town of Southeast, New York, has long been known as the location of a high level of paranormal activity. Reports of sightings are quite common, from the reservoir in Southeast to the Tilly Foster mine pit in Brewster, New York.

Nancy and Roger, residents of an area nearby, have become increasingly interested in stories of the strange lights seen near the mines on the lonely dirt road called Reservoir Road. Whenever the opportunity permitted, they spent their evenings watching for anything supernatural or strange. Nancy's first unusual experience in the area occurred when she was with Roger. As they drove along the road, their minds seemed to be elsewhere, until Roger heard a suspicious noise. Nancy remembers that she didn't really believe he heard a noise; she thought he was playing a joke. Roger got out of the car to investigate. While he was gone, she started to feel a bit spooked. Attributing this feeling to nerves, she suddenly turned to where Roger would have been sitting and saw a depression in the car seat cushion. When he returned, he opened the car door, leaned in the car, and asked her if she smelled "it." She became increasingly uncomfortable, and had no idea what he was talking about. Although this behavior was strange and inconsistent with his personality, she was still convinced that this was part of a sneaky scheme to trick her. He insisted that she answer his question, and repeatedly asked if she smelled "the lilacs." In an attempt to end the chaos, she stepped out of the car to please him and attempted to smell the supposed "lilacs." Much to Roger's disappointment, Nancy did not smell anything. It wasn't until she got back into the car that she smelled the overpowering scent of flowers—specifically, lilacs.

Their second strange encounter that evening again occurred while they were driving. Roger had stopped the car at the south end of the road. Suddenly, they both heard a boom-like explosion that vibrated the car. After parking the car, they got out to see if they could determine the source of the noise. Within five minutes of hearing the explosion, they walked up a hill to survey their surroundings, but still couldn't determine the cause of the loud sound. When they returned to the parked car, Nancy saw what she at first thought was a tank with bright lights making a turn over the crest of a hill. As the object silently glided directly toward them, it seemed to be only a few feet above the ground. They realized that the dirt road they were on wasn't very wide, and there was no room for the unknown vehicle to go around them. Roger frantically started the car, put it in reverse, and backed out until he reached the main road. Nancy vividly remembers looking out the back window and seeing it following them as they rounded their first turn. After the turn, it was gone. It seemed almost impossible to them that an object of that size could just vanish into thin air. They continued down the road and back to the main thoroughfare, then returned to the site where they had heard the noise. However, the mysterious vehicle was nowhere in sight. Nancy and Roger could find no sign that would lead them to a logical conclusion. The object never returned, and their experience remained a mystery.

Other unusual sightings have been reported in the area around the Tilly Foster Mine. Since the late 1890s, generations of residents have seen what most describe as a round, yellow (sometimes white) light the diameter of a basketball. Residents have attempted to explain these lights as the ghosts of the miners who died in the late 1800s when the mine caved in, since it wasn't until shortly after the accident that the mysterious lights appeared.

During the summer of 1993, one of Phil's associates, a physicist in New Jersey, proposed a theory. He suggested that phenomena like the "ghost lights" of Reservoir Road are rarely seen or not seen most of the time because they may often be invisible to the naked eye. He suggested that if blue-sensitive film was used in conjunction with a dark blue filter, the light might be visible in photographs. Phil's assistance was requested. However, hanging out until all hours of the summer night on some lonely, dark road didn't appeal to Phil. After all, the odds against seeing something were astronomical. He declined. Nevertheless, the physicist who proposed the theory set up a camera with special film on a tripod, ready to shoot anything that looked remotely strange. The following is his description of what took place that night, as told to us several days after his encounter with the ghost of Reservoir Road.

"I got to the location at 10:00 P.M. on May 21, 1994. I drove around for a while and finally decided to park on the far end of lower Magnetic Mine Road, which for some reason is marked on the map as part of Reservoir Road. I set up the camera, loaded it with the special blue film, and waited. About an hour passed. I began to feel uneasy, as if I was being watched. I thought it was nothing more than being on this lonely, dark road where people have reported seeing UFOs, alien creatures, and ghosts. Then I looked down the dirt road and saw what looked like a fog. The fog formed a sphere that was, I would say, about two feet in diameter. As I watched, it began to pulsate. I shot a number of frames. I got curious and started to approach the cloud. As I got closer to the cloud it slowly moved away, keeping its distance from me.

"I went back to the camera and the ball of fog started to approach me. It was about 150 feet away. Then it moved up and down, covering a span of about five feet or less. As I watched, it started vibrating and began to change color. The change was barely noticeable, and I hoped that I would get something on film. This went on for about ten minutes. Then the light just vanished. When I got the film developed I was surprised to see that the images came out so bright. I guess I was right when I suspected that the phenomenon radiates at the violet end of the spectrum."

We were quite amazed at the images that were recorded on this film. In one of the frames, the object seems to be

Plate 12. The spook light seen on Magnetic Mine Road. Is this a form of the UFO phenomenon, or the ghosts of miners who died in a cave-in?

ionizing the air around it, creating a cloud. We know from past experience that UFOs have been known to do this. The light also changed color, indicating that the frequency of the energy that was released also changed. The photographer actually photographed the spooks light of Reservoir Road, called by old-time residents the ghost of the mine.

Typically, experiences such as these are viewed as problematic or frightening. More often, paranormal reports like the two described above are rarely reported because the witnesses fear ridicule. Although people who encounter strange phenomena are very interested in finding out what it was that they saw, it is curious how many fail to take the opportunity to investigate these strange happenings. Many residents in the area who have reported paranormal activity chose to ignore their experiences out of fear, hoping someone would come up with a logical explanation. Although we are sensitive to this issue, hearing these reports made us eager to research the matter and find some answers.

We started with the basics. Before physically searching for clues, we researched basic information on the Tilly Foster and Brewster mines in the Brewster Museum and the New York City Public Library. We spent hours looking at early mine journals on microfilm and making copies of old diagrams and other important technical information.

We were looking for answers that went beyond opinion or, more accurately, answers that might appear contradictory or absurd, but could have meaning nonetheless. Many ancient myths suggest that treasures are found where least expected. As we accepted the challenge to physically explore the paranormal activity in the area around the mines, we often questioned whether finding the the answers was worth risking our safety. Nevertheless, we continued to probe into the depths of the past and placed ourselves in dangerous situations to try and find what we least expected. It soon became clear that researching allowed us the opportunity to embark upon a journey that not only heightened self-awareness, but offered an understanding of the past that could unlock the doors of the present.

Probing into the Depths of the Past

The history and construction of a mine can explain some of the mysteries that have been reported. The Tilly Foster Mine is an open-pit mine. It is filled with mazes of underground shafts lined with iron ore. The intricate mazes lead into curious galleries that were originally constructed to remove the ore systematically. By 1885, the mine had reached a depth of more than 600 feet, fifty stories below ground level. The lower mine consisted of underground shafts leading into galleries where pillars of ore twenty feet wide were left in place to support the ceiling at each level. However, it became increasingly difficult to bring ore up from the lower levels, and water seepage was becoming a problem. At first, many thought the water came from the Middle Branch Reservoir but, after emptying the reservoir, water continued to seep into the mine. To this day no one can explain where the water comes from. By March, 1889, Tilly Foster had been converted into an open-pit mine with a funnel-shaped pit 450 feet long by 300 feet wide at the top and reaching 170 feet into the earth.

The miners continued to dig deeper and widen the pit until the last part of 1895, when the mine was 500 feet wide at the top and had reached a depth of 400 feet. However, the ore bed lay at a steep angle and had many faults running through it. The heedless extraction of ore ultimately precipitated the end of mining at Tilly Foster. On November 29, 1895, several hundred tons of rock broke loose and knocked thirty-four men into the pit. Thirteen men were killed in the cave-in; the rest survived. Ten of the bodies were pulled from the mine before night fell, when the operation was suspended. It took weeks to find the remaining three men, whose lives were only known by a number. It is said that, to this day, these three men haunt upper and lower Magnetic Mine Road and Reservoir Road, from the town Southeast to the area of downtown Brewster. Needless to say, the tragedy had a solemn effect on the mining community. After the accident, the mine continued to flood, and it was closed permanently in August, 1897.

The mine was supposedly inactive until 1925, when a road material company began taking gravel from it. Since then it is evident that the United States government used the deep, water-filled pit for underwater testing. What other uses the government had for the mines and what they found inside is unknown, but we will explore some of the possibilities below.

Exploring into the Depths of the Unknown: Hidden Bases?

Underground bases in the mine area became our focus after we discovered that the government had conducted tests around the mines. There was also a news clipping from 1967 that talked about a certain unknown government agency buying the property around the mines in Brewster and nearby Putnam Valley and Lake Carmel. In addition, our interviews and research had led us to our next task—to find the secret entrance to the underground base that may have been used by the government for underground UFO studies. As mentioned in chapter 8, Phil did some exploration of this area in 1989 and was asked to leave. In the summer of 1995, we returned to the site, intent on finding the truth, risking possible arrest for trespassing in the highly secured area. To our surprise, no gates blocked our way and no security stopped us at the perimeter.

Nothing came easily for us. For some reason, maps of the area were in short supply or nonexistent. It seemed that many files at the Putnam County Historical Society were missing or misplaced. Even the historian for the town did not know the exact location of the mine entrances. Most of our exploration had to be done blindly, on foot. Hiking through the back woods of Putnam County, we spent several days looking for answers. Finally, we discovered that the area was no longer guarded and free for us to explore.

Our first find was the house that Phil had observed years before. Judging from the remains left in the house, the occupants seemed to have left in quite a hurry. A calendar, a Danbury, Connecticut newspaper, and several phone books had been left behind, allowing us to determine the last occupancy date to be 1990. We had already determined that the occupants had taken only what they deemed necessary when they left, but the collection of items that remained was a bizarre array of things. For example, outside was a street lamp in the middle of nowhere, and enough private telephone equipment to make the local phone company, who had no records of its existence, envious. There were also a number of power boxes that boosted up to 100 amps, speakers, receivers, radio equipment, and an alarm system that protected the entire house and perimeter. In the yard area we found an old Army-issue tent from 1950 that was big enough to sleep eight comfortably, a fifteen-foot collinear radio communication antenna, four rolls of heavy-duty high voltage electric cable and, in one of the sheds, an entire welding setup. It was peculiar that the items were all old, as if someone had raided a huge warehouse of goods and taken items that would not be missed. The dusty clothes we found were fairly new, similar to what a mechanic or laborer would wear. We also found several pairs of expensive, new-looking work boots. We began to realize anything was possible, so we continued looking. As we entered the basement we found two sets of stairs that led nowhere. It was impossible to tell if the stairways had been blocked off at the end; to get that far we would have needed an excavation team. A further perimeter sweep uncovered a well (or something that looked like a well), hidden under a roof-like structure with a fence around it. It was at least twenty or twenty-five feet in diameter and appeared to have been electrified at one time.

Everything we found added more questions without offering any apparent answers. According to the maps we had brought, this area was supposed to have at least one mine entrance, if not two or three. Searching the area proved to be harder than we thought. We were left with no choice but to follow a complex maze of paths, covered with undergrowth.

Trudging through the brush, we had started to question whether it was worth continuing when we came across an old cement-block structure. Viewed through the trees, it looked quite out of place and caught our attention. It turned out to be a long, deep pit; the cement building above it was some sort of base for cables and machinery. This first discovery brought us off the road and into the thick of the woods. From there we spotted another structure through the trees. This object was a set of four cement-like silos, connected together. Each had an opening through which we could enter, and a roof about fifteen-feet high with a square hole in the middle. After some prodding we were able to determine that each silo may once have extended underground. Now, however, a cement floor covered the original hole. Near the silos was an old smelter and another very large, long wall of unknown use. Now we knew for sure that we were in the right area, and on the way to finding the entrances to the mines.

After days of searching in the hot summer sun, we came across an area toward which we felt drawn. The trail curved around the edge of a lake, then led us up and down over tree roots and rocks. Suddenly, we found our treasure. As we approached the side of a hill, we discovered a gaping hole that seemed to stare back at us. The wide entrance was partly covered by a rusty, decrepit chain link fence that looked as if it had been violently torn open. For our own professional purposes we referred to our discovery as the "monster cave." However, after more research, we learned that the monster cave was actually the Hattfield Adit or Pit. We carefully checked the area and proceeded to enter the rugged opening. Because we had not yet found any caves, mines, or openings, we were unprepared. We had with us only a small flashlight that didn't adequately reveal the contents of the interior. However, it looked like the cave contained a large pool of shallow water. We decided to come back with suitable equipment so that we could better explore the area.

Still motivated to find the elusive mine entrances, we continued our journey. Almost ready to give up, we were heading back toward the car, when we once again found ourselves drawn up a particular path. We decided this would be our last attempt. The message of ancient myths proved true; we found another treasure where we least expected it. In the fading light, as we walked up the lonely, desolate road, we came across several interesting surprises. The first was a very strange shed, almost like a trailer set up on cinder blocks, with shelves for storage inside. There were also large holes that looked like caved-in pits, but unlike some of the others we had found, these had no water in them.

Wind Cave

As we continued down the road, the air suddenly started to get cold. We rounded a corner and encountered another sharp drop in temperature. An amphitheater had been constructed in the side of a very large mountain, and a gaping hole was centered in the middle. Trees growing on the side of the amphitheater gave testimony that it had not been built yesterday, but decades ago. Looking into the entrance, we saw a billowing mist pouring out of the darkness, into the rest of the world. After a short walk across some loose rocks we reached the opening, where we noticed a drop in temperature of at least fifteen degrees. Armed with little more than a penlight, we were unable to see more than a few feet into the mist. We called this latest discovery "Wind Cave." Our curiosity certainly was piqued and we wanted to know more. We knew we needed to come back with the appropriate supplies to continue our exploration.

The next week, equipped with a high-powered flashlight, we went back to the site. We entered the area from a different direction, and were amazed at how many paths cut through the countryside. Monster Cave was our first destination. Flashing the light along the wall, we saw that the mine went back about 150 to 200 feet. The ceiling maintained a pretty even height above the surface of the water. Some rock and roll symbols on the back wall gave us the impression that the water wasn't too deep. On our next visit we would bring waders.

We then ventured into Wind Cave. After descending a steep slope, we were able to walk about the same distance inside before we encountered a pool of water about fifteen feet deep. The flashlight was unable to penetrate the mist that

Plate 13. Inside Wind Cave.

came billowing out from the far reaches of the cave. This gave us the impression that it went back a very long way. The wall on the left side went back and curved around to form this large opening, then returned to the main passage thirty feet farther down. We were unable to see into the main passage, which curved out of sight.

While we were investigating these two mines, we were also still looking for the Brewster Mine. Again we found ourselves in an area without a proper map, wandering through heavy growth, looking for a mine. This time proved no different than the last; as we finished our day of exploration, we chose to follow a path based on feeling. After walking through the overgrowth for a few minutes, we came across a huge chasm cut into the side of the hill. It was a gapping slash that ran down the length of the side of the mountain. Looking down into the cut, we could see an opening on the opposite end. Although it had been closed with cement blocks, someone had removed just enough of them to squeeze through. We crossed the chasm on a fallen log, and proceeded down its side. This expedition took place before we had outfitted ourselves with the proper supplies, including lights. After climbing down a log and dropping down onto some rocks, we came face to face with a dark opening, and we were unable to see any distance inside.

Our search no longer offered the thrills of a treasure hunt. Instead, it had turned into a rather frustrating, tedious process. Phil threw a few rocks into the opening to determine if there was any water. Although it seemed clear to enter, without the proper equipment this was impossible. However, now we knew the locations of all the mines we had heard about, and could decide on our next move.

Several days later, we returned to the Brewster area and began our exploration of Monster Cave. We carried our waders to the site, got dressed, and entered the cave. After five steps, the water was already up to our hips, dangerously close to the limit of our waders. Looking ahead with our lights, the crystal clear water did not appear to be as deep as we now knew it was. Because we could go no further that day, we packed up and headed over to Wind Cave. Once we got there, we again donned our waders and proceeded to walk down into the dark bowels of the earth.

Going In

The mist was thick as we entered the dismal mine, and we could not see very far into the distance. There was writing on the wall that was easily visible from our vantage point in the water. Phil was able to translate some of the symbols and language painted on the walls. It was clear that the cave's previous visitors thought they were worshipping the anti-Christ. They referred to the mine and tunnel as the gateway to hell.

As we had suspected from our initial survey, the first tunnel on the right came to an immediate dead end. The tunnel on the left wrapped around and formed a grotto, with a beach. A path led up the side, which was very difficult to maneuver in our bulky waders. After climbing around the corner we found it was a dead end.

We returned to the main passage and continued down into the mist. On this trip we had brought along a another person, Karen, who could go for help if anything happened to us. We also had walkie talkies so we could stay in touch, and used a rope to connect ourselves to Karen before we went in. Marianne held onto the rope as Phil went down the main passage alone. Silt swirled around our feet, turning the clear water into a muddy, orange-red, that obscured the bottom. We used rods that Phil had fashioned to make sure our footing was solid before we took each step.

The rope we had gotten was only a hundred feet long. When Marianne reached the end, she had to make a decision: go on without it, or stay while Phil went ahead. Marianne dropped the rope into the water and followed him. The mist cleared as we got farther into the mine, and we were able to make out a wall of cement blocks in front of us, to our left. Directly above the front block was an entrance to another area, but it was 35 feet in the air! Both walls in the main channel had been broken through, forming a passage to the other side. However, we went straight in, past the side tunnel, and continued down the main tunnel until we could no longer see the entrance. The water seemed to get deeper and we had lost radio contact with Karen. We came to the conclusion that we would need the raft to go farther, so we turned around and proceeded back to the main tunnel.

Our next adventure took us back into the Brewster Mine. Armed with the rope and our backup, Karen, we went in. This mine was not wet, but the climb down was very steep. We used the rope to secure our footing and headed down into the darkness. The tunnel turned and twisted, and we followed it in as far as our rope would allow. Our 100-foot rope ended about 10 feet short of a pit. We were able to look over the edge, and found a 15-foot drop. A small tunnel was located at the right bottom corner of the pit. It was only a crawl space; without going down there we would not know where it went. As we turned to walk back up, Marianne began to slide downward into the darkness. Phil, still holding the rope, extended his arm and grabbed her before she slid off the edge into the pit. Marianne then used Phil as an extension of the rope and climbed over him to safety.

A raft provided the next step in our investigation. Our next journey into Monster Cave was afloat. We loaded ourselves onto the raft for our first trip. It turned out that the curve in the back, which we thought was a tunnel, turned out to be a dead end. We were surprised, however, by how deep the water really was! We had expected it to be about ten feet deep, but the actual depth turned out to be over thirty feet! For the first trip in our raft, we floated along with thirty feet of crystal clear water below us. After our initial sweep, we went back to take a look at what was under the water. The flashlight revealed that the mine floor went down at a very steep angle from the entrance all the way to the back. There was no evidence of tunnels under the water.

Toward the end of summer we returned to Wind Cave with the eight-foot inflatable raft. Entering the opening and descending the slope into the water, we continued where we had left off on our last ex-pedition. We started out in the raft but soon realized that the water level must have dropped due to the drought we had experienced over the summer. We were able to walk around comfortably, pulling the raft behind us. Our previous trip had ended at a curve. Now we walked around it and, to our surprise, the silt

Plate 14. Photograph of Monster Cave. If there was once an underground entrance here, it has been sealed by water. The authors had to raft into the cave, since the water was over thirty feet deep.

we had been walking in became mud, then dirt. We were also surprised to find that we had been walking on an old railbed the whole way. Seeing it laid out before us made us realize what had been under our feet, in the silt. Strange noises caused us to pause and take a look around. We were unable to locate the cause of the sounds, so we continued on. In the distance we were able to make out another wall. As we got closer we could see that there was an opening large enough for us to enter. The ground on the other side of the wall was littered with discarded papers. It was difficult to tell what this area really was. A steep climb up wet and slippery rocks brought us into a crossroads of tunnels.

Plate 15. Photograph inside Wind Cave. The authors had to explore the mine in a raft.

We split up and checked out all the different passages. One of them led to the outside. We had found the back door, a straight vertical climb up more wet, slippery rocks. This passage seemed to be a dead end, and we headed back. Phil thought that we should call it a day, but Marianne wanted to finish exploring the remaining passages. We picked up the raft where we had left it and headed to the first side tunnel we had seen halfway in from the entrance. The tunnel wound around the corner, getting smaller the farther we walked. It led back a few hundred yards, then seemed to reach a dead end like the others. We returned to the main passage, and the last area left to explore.

The Upper Level

We went back through the first cinderblock wall, made a sharp right turn, and entered a large cavern. We could smell some kind of gas and saw a log with a piece of cloth wrapped around it. This seemed to be the source of the fumes. We guessed that whoever came into the mine to make the drawings on the walls had left their torch floating in the water. We continued past the log. So far, most of the water had been the same depth, with little or no variance. This cove was similar to the other in size and shape, but portions of it were very deep. Many pieces of broken wood were sticking up out of the water, so we couldn't take the raft in. It took some maneuvering to get through to the little beach. We finally made it and climbed up the hill. A rope left behind by someone else helped us up a steep incline. The upper level of the chamber branched out to the left and right. The passage to the right seemed to lead to another exit or entrance. The left path looked as if it might lead to another tunnel. Following the twists and turns, we were disappointed to find that it reached a dead end in a little stage-like area.

Our exploration of the interior of the mine seemed to be finished. We still wanted to walk the surface to see if we could find any entrances to the rest of the mine that may have been closed off. We needed to come back again, anyway, to finish taking the pictures we wanted.

On our next visit we walked around the exterior of Wind Cave. The mine was very long, and we wanted to know if there were any unmarked passages or entrances. We had brought the walkie talkies, so we split up and walked across what we hoped was the top of the mine. We came across what we thought was the little entrance from the upper level we had found during our last trip. Continuing our search, we came across the back entrance and, to our surprise, an unmarked tunnel on the other side. It appeared to be an unconnected continuance of the other mine. Our objective that day had been to wrap things up; instead, we just seemed to open another can of worms.

Meanwhile, we had purchased an additional rope to take into the Brewster Mine. It was autumn and, since the leaves had all fallen off the trees, the whole area we wanted to explore was easier to see. Employees of Putnam County, who were now using "Marvin's house," would be able to see our movements. We didn't think that the county wanted to take responsibility for people poking around, so we had to very careful. We were able to get in without being noticed, except by a barking dog.

The weather had changed; it was very cold on this trip. The mine, however, was warm, almost hot. We headed back down to the area we had started to explore before. Now, with our additional rope, we would be able to continue past the point where we had stopped and see what was down there. Reaching the fifteen-foot drop, Phil descended the sheer wall. We wondered why the wall would be sheer in an old mine. He went through the hole in the wall on his hands and knees. The low passage opened up, then dropped. Throwing the rope over the edge, Phil went down another fifteen to twenty feet. Although he was attacked by bats, he was able to look down and see that the passage continued to drop another fifteen feet or so, then intersected a tunnel that ran horizontally to the left and right. Phil dropped a rock and counted three seconds before he heard it splash into water—it had fallen about ninety feet before it hit water that filled the pit in the darkness below him. He pulled himself back up and reported to me. He had seen a few water moccasins slipping along the lower tunnel. In the 1800s they did not have the capability to blast sheer, very smooth walls, so this area puzzled us greatly. Also, this shaft and tunnel were not shown in the original cross-section of the mine. This only made the entire situation more mysterious. What was down there?

Frustrated by our inability to get down into the Brewster Mine, we returned the other site, determined to take our pictures and check out the new tunnel. A colleague of ours, Fred Dennis, had loaned us a high-intensity searchlight and a couple of battery packs. This lit up the interior as if it was daylight. We got into Wind Cave without incident and rafted along smoothly. We took pictures and went to reexamine that upper level opening, to see if it visually matched what we had seen outside. It didn't. Part of the reason we were so curious was that we had seen a shaft going straight down some distance, and another tunnel branching off in two directions. We had discovered an entrance from the outside that did not connect with anything on the inside!

Heading back out, we returned to Monster Cave to look around with the powerful light. We took the raft onto the pool and dropped a rock tied with twine to measure the depth. We had been right; it was about 30 feet. A canoe had sunk to the bottom of the pool; it was eerie to see a dead boat laying on the bottom at a incredibly steep angle, but it clearly showed the depth change. A sweep with the big flashlight didn't reveal anything else, so we wrote this mine off as being nothing more than a mine.

Now we headed to the back entrance and the new tunnel with great excitement. Without delay we got ready and went in. This tunnel was too small and narrow to accommodate the raft. The going was rough. The entrance was rocky, and the silt was very deep. Every step stirred it up so that you couldn't see the bottom. A few hundred yards in we saw beautiful iron ore stalactites, an iron ore waterfall, and incredible ribbon formations. It was really breathtaking. Our next surprise was to find that the end of the tunnel had originally been shored up with a wooden beam, but had been closed off by a cave-in. The thoroughness of the job on this unmarked passage gave us the feeling that it had been done on purpose.

Had we really found the mines that were reported to contain the secret bases? If we had, someone had done a pretty good job of covering the evidence. However, there still were some very strange discrepancies. As of now, we have not fully explored the Brewster Mine, but our initial survey shows that it was worked long after it was reported to have been closed down. Questions still remain. Who used the mine and created the new extensions of these tunnels? For what purpose? Exploration of this mine is very difficult. It will take a great deal more planning before this underground world can be explored fully. What Phil saw, while dangling off the side of the ledge, did not match the diagrams and maps of this mine. Whoever was down there had done a very good job of covering up their tracks so that they would not be discovered.

CHAPTER TEN ...

SWITCH

When we finished exploring the underground mines in Putnam County, we realized that whoever might have been there several years before had now left. We feel that there still may be some activity in Brewster Mine, but since the lower levels are flooded with water it will be some time before we can fully explore that area. We hope that in the near future we will be able to update our research and write a full report of the current activity taking place in the mysterious Brewster Mine.

If the alien intelligence, or whatever operation was once underground in Putnam County, was gone, where did it go? Our next task was to look for an area in which the sighting of UFOs has increased and continues at a steady rate. Our attention was drawn to Pine Bush, New York. Since the eighties, encounters of many types have occurred there. Pine Bush is located just west of the Hudson River, at the base of the Catskill Mountains. It was once a small farming community, and the residents had no interest at all in UFOs or other strange phenomena. This changed after many reliable people in the town had encounters with the unknown that profoundly changed their lives. During our research in that area, we also learned that there are a number of underground caves and mines in the vicinity. On more than one occasion, local residents reported seeing government vehicles and military troops near these underground entrances, and entering them. It seemed to us that we may have found the base for the new operation.

The Pine Bush sightings are documented in the book *Silent Invasion,* by Ellen Crystal. Ellen spent considerable time investigating and trying to document the phenomenon taking place there. However, special credit for shedding light on the happenings at Pine Bush must go to Dawn Lay, a local resident of that area. Dawn started monthly meetings at the VFW hall for people who had had a UFO experience and wanted to talk about it. In June of 1995, Phil was asked to speak at one of these meetings. He was very surprised at the number of people who showed up. After his presentation, he asked those who had had a UFO experience to put their names on a list and give a brief description of their encounters. To his surprise, forty percent of those who attended the meeting either put their names on the list or contacted us later. Phil was also a little taken aback when most of the experiences seemed to be possible contact cases.

In this chapter, we will present two very interesting case studies. Since our research in Pine Bush and nearby Ellenville and Newburgh is still ongoing, our readers are invited to write to us to request an update.

Your Friends Are Here!

Our first case study involved a young couple, who we will refer to as Maria and George. Maria and George both had a history with paranormal phenomena before they met each other, but the number of incidents escalated after they got married. Maria remembers that, as a child, she used to see "ghosts" around her father. Sometimes the ghosts visited her at night and took her away. During her teen years, after a visit from the ghosts, Maria suddenly developed an eye twitch. Her mom took her to the doctor, who uncovered a piece of silicone embedded in her lower eyelid. The doctor was very puzzled as to how it could have gotten there.

George had a much more active childhood when it came to strange phenomena. At a very early age he started having recurring dreams of strange places and structures. The dreams were so vivid that he would draw the things he saw when he woke up in the morning. He always had a fascination with pyramids, since he often saw them in his dreams. The pyramids were so real that he was compelled to try to build one. It was as if a telepathic message had been placed in his mind, so that he was obsessed to construct what he saw. A friend who also had a fascination with pyramids approached George shortly after his dream. Although George did not tell this person about his dream, the friend insisted that they work together to construct a large pyramid of glass and metal. Although the pyramid was never constructed, George still wanted to build one, so he began to put together a number of tiny ones.

While growing up, George had two UFO sightings, during which he saw strange lights in the sky perform amazing acrobatic flights. He felt that the sightings were staged for him, and that there was some type of telepathic connection between him and the UFOs. After he met Maria, he tried to forget about the UFOs and other strange occurrences that he had experienced all his life. However, now and then something would happen to remind him that he was somehow connected to this unknown intelligence that has been around him since his childhood. It wasn't until he married Maria that both their lives took a very bizarre turn.

George feels that he has been chosen by an alien intelligence to perform some function in the future. He was told in a dream that they will come for him and take him away "when the stars fall out of the sky." The couple claim that, since they have been married, a number of small gray beings with very large eyes have come into their home on numerous occasions and abducted them. After the visits, Maria and George wake up in the morning feeling very tired, but they have never found any marks on their bodies. This has been going on for so long now that George feels that he can predict when they are going to have a visit from the alien creatures, because his body will start to "tingle." The visitations have been so frequent that when Maria sees the beings she says to George, "Your friends are here." She says this because George actually feels that the beings mean him no harm and have come to help him.

George and Maria have a daughter who is almost two years old. One day, she brought out her doll and asked her mom to open its head. Maria asked her where she had seen something like that and she told her mom, "They do it to Daddy at night." The child has also pointed to pictures of alien beings on book and magazine covers and indicated that this is what she has seen enter the house. Like most people who are experiencing paranormal phenomena, electromagnetic disturbances also take place in their home. Clocks do not work properly, light bulbs explode, and appliances malfunction for no apparent reason. Stranger still, the phone rings several times during the day and night with nobody on the line, although sometimes a strange beeping sound is heard. Although they have caller ID, the mysterious caller's number never appears on the ID readout.

Before George was married, he lived with a friend. One evening, as this friend left the house, he saw blue globes of light enter the window to George's room. Also, on more than one occasion he saw these blue lights enter George's sleeping body. After Maria and George got married, the lights did not go away. They both saw them at least once a week, flying around their apartment and going right through the windows and the wall.

George and Maria have been abducted a number of times. The scenario is always the same. The beings enter their bedroom, then approach them. The next thing they know, it is morning. After reviewing the case, and hours of audio tape, we have come to the conclusion that the alien intelligence seems to be more interested in Maria than in George. Maria had more of a recollection of seeing the beings than George did. George seems to be in mental contact with the intelligence, and while Maria is fearful of the beings, George is not. The intelligence could be using George to keep Maria calm so that the abduction can take place without any problems. The big question is, why are they so interested in Maria? We can speculate on this, but will leave the final conclusion up to our readers.

Why Me?

The next case study is interesting, but very complex. It involves a woman named Laura, who has had a great deal of paranormal phenomena take place in her life ever since she was a child. When Laura was only five years old, she had an "imaginary" friend who lived in the wall of her room. She talked to her friend, and faithfully left food for it every night. She always found the food gone in the morning. She was sure that her friend came out of the wall late at night and ate the food, but now guesses that her parents removed it in the morning. Laura still thinks it was strange that her mother never asked her to stop leaving the food in a dish near the wall. Later, when she got older and asked about it, her mother seemed to have no knowledge of the food-by-the-wall incidents.

Like most people who have contact with this alien intelligence throughout their lives, as a child Laura woke up in the middle of the night and saw strange beings enter her room. She called them "witches." These so-called witches were very tall and skinny, with long faces and dark eyes. They had the ability to disappear into thin air whenever her mother came running into the room after she heard Laura scream. The beings entered her room from the closet area at least two to three times a week, and continued to visit her until she was a teenager. Many times, she would be unable to move and would have the feeling of being taken to some place outside her home. However, she has little conscious recollection of what took place at that time. Since these strange nighttime visitations, Laura has had difficulty sleeping. Even as an adult she sleeps only four hours a night. Today, she is in her forties and has a thirteen-year-old daughter. Contact with this alien intelligence seems to be increasing.

When Laura does sleep, a multitude of images enter her mind. In some cases, she claims that she can predict the future. She has seen things like plane crashes; in the vision she sometimes is able to see the numbers on the plane. Then, within the next few days she would hear of a plane crash on TV and learn that the flight number, or the plane ID number, matched the number she had seen in her dream. Laura always found this type of experience frustrating and disheartening. She knew something terrible was going to happen, but she could do nothing to stop it. She also has a talent for finding things that people have lost, and sometimes knew the thoughts of others. This is one of the common threads that we found in all contact cases—just about all contactees are born with psychic abilities. The alien intelligence seems to be very interested in these people, and might be keeping them under some type of close surveillance.

The earliest actual UFO sighting that Laura could remember took place when she was nine years old. She and her friends were playing on a dead-end street, and a large UFO appeared out of nowhere and hovered above the trees. Although her friends ran home, screaming, Laura stood and watched the object by herself. Later, her mother joined her. Mother and daughter watched the object for about half an hour. Laura had no fear of the UFO; instead, she had the feeling that it was there to take her home. She remembers the sighting vividly to this day. She described the object as being very large, disk-shaped, with a set of white blinking lights on the bottom. This sighting occurred in late spring at about five or six in the evening, so she was able to make out the understructure. The UFO then moved off without a sound, and shot away at great speed.

When Laura was ten, she had her tonsils removed. She wasn't afraid of the hospital, but once they put her on the operating table, she looked up and saw the lights and became terrified. To this day, bright lights placed above her head make her feel very uneasy. There is no doubt that Laura is remembering some aspect of her many abductions. There are many cases in which people who were abducted claim that they were put on a table with bright lights above them. Like most people who have contact experiences, Laura has been plagued by all sorts of electromagnetic disturbances. On more than one occasion, all the clocks in the house have stopped at 3:15 A.M. We found this very interesting, because the majority of UFO cases classified as High Strangeness take place between two and four in the morning.

During her adult life, Laura continued to have UFO sightings. In 1982, while driving home on I-84 in New-burgh, New York, Laura, her husband, and their two chil-dren were shocked to see an immense UFO appear out of the clouds. It was about nine in the evening in the early summer; the sky was quite dark. They pulled over to the side of the highway, and Laura and the two children got out of the car. Her husband did not get out. He just sat in the car, almost unresponsive to what was taking place. Laura told us, "It was like he was in some type of trance." As they watched the UFO, they realized that it was very low in the sky, and that there was a sort of cloud around it. Laura told us that it was so huge, it was like " a floating city." They were right underneath it. They could see frosted windows around the craft, and shadows moving around inside the windows.

The huge ship, made up of a silver gray metal, made no noise. As they watched, a beam of blue light shot down from the object to the left and right of where they were standing. Then, without warning, two smaller ships about one-tenth the size of the larger one, came out of nowhere and did three fly-bys around the big ship. The smaller objects were triangular in shape and had blue and green lights. The large ship ascended slowly, followed by the smaller ones. After this sighting, Laura and her daughter began to experience many unusual phenomena, including poltergeist activity and a multitude of abductions by the alien intelligence.

The beings tormented Laura so much that she sought help. She was told of an Indian shaman who lived in Arizona. This person understood these beings and how to deal with them so, in the late eighties, she went to meet him. What took place is one of the most unusual stories we have heard in our combined twenty-five years of research into the paranormal. The shaman, known to Laura as "Jade," told her that she would have to go through a special ritual called "soul retrieval." Jade felt that the beings had a part of her life force. He and Laura would leave their bodies and confront the entities to bargain for the return of Laura's soul.

As the ritual began, Jade tied a rope around Laura and took her hand. He admonished her not to let go; he felt that the beings were very powerful, and that it was going to be very difficult to confront them. Laura told us that they both left their bodies. She remembers flying through the sky, holding on to Jade. They continued to travel, passed through a door, and found themselves on a ship. Three beings were standing in a room. They were very tall, and had long arms. They seemed to be covered in a silvery glow. They had no hair; their heads were round on the top and pointed at the chin. This gave their faces a very non-human, angular appearance. Laura said that the shape of their heads remind-ed her of the "witches" who used to come into her room at night when she was a child. As she stood there in awe, Jade seemed to argue with the beings. He asked them to return a part of Laura, a part that they had possessed since she was born. The beings said that they were from the Pleiades, and had been with Laura's family for generations. They also said that they were in contact with her grandmother and mother, and now they were starting contact with her daughter.

When Laura was younger she lost a baby. The beings told her that the baby did not die—they had it now, because it was one of theirs. Then a human-looking woman brought out a baby for her to see. She thought it was the one she "lost," except that it was much too young. The baby looked almost human, but looked more like the beings in the room. The woman took Laura farther into the ship, into a large brightly lit, oval room. It was filled from top to bottom with rows of cylindrical canisters. Each canister was full of a bub-bling liquid in which a baby was suspended. All of the infants appeared to be of the same age.

Then Laura opened her eyes and was back in her body. She remembered every part of her ordeal. The shaman told her that in all of his years of helping people, he had never been aboard a ship. The ritual seemed to have been in vain. When Laura arrived home the sightings of strange lights and beings did not stop. Now, even her young daughter seems to be part of her contact experience. Laura's daughter is unusually inquisitive for her age. While other children are more concerned with the ice cream flavor of the month and hanging out at the mall, she is more interested in reading books on different religions and philosophy. She also claims to be in some type of mental contact with a female entity that she refers to as "Troy." Troy has told her that she has been chosen for a special purpose and that, although there are many things that seem bad in her life now, things will get better. Like the other female members of her family in previous generations, it is clear that this young girl is the next in line for contact with the alien intelligence.

These are only two of the many cases that have come to our attention. The great majority of these people seem to be drawn to the Pine Bush area of New York. Why this is so, we can't say. Is it coincidence, or by design? Recently, that area has drawn many so-called researchers from all over the east coast. Some of these so-called UFO investigators are even stranger than the aliens. As time goes on, it seems that a serious scientific investigation of this phenomenon is being replaced by paranoia and fanciful dreams. In the past, it was often thought that people who saw UFOs were crazy. Judging from the many people we have met, it may be the UFO investigators who have a few screws loose.

The alien intelligence now seems to be operating in Ulster and Orange Counties of New York. Although some of the Pine Bush sightings are nothing more than the imaginations of bored people, a good number of cases still defy explanation. We were shown a number of videos that were supposed to be of UFOs, taken in Pine Bush. There was no doubt that these videos showed nothing more than jet aircraft in a landing pattern for Stewart Airport. The person who shot the video insisted that the images were UFOs, even though one could clearly make out the outline of the jet and hear its engine noise. When it was evident that they were planes, the "true believers" in the Pine Bush area said, "Well, the ships can take different shapes and look like planes or jets." If this were true, we could never know for sure whether we were looking at a plane or a UFO. Sometimes, when we want very much to believe, we do not learn anything—we only fool ourselves.

In regard to the underground operations in that area, we do believe that some type of government installation exists. Perhaps it is UFO-related, but we don't know for sure, since most of our data from that area come from secondary sources. We did, however, interview several people who independently claim that they were abducted and taken into an underground complex. There they saw beings who had very long faces with white skin. Most of the time these creatures were seen operating machinery, and were involved in some type of drilling operation. It is going to be difficult to find out what is really going on in Ulster and Orange Counties. At the present time, it is impossible to tell the "signal from the noise."

CHAPTER ELEVEN

THE BURDEN OF PROOF

By the time researchers have been investigating paranormal phenomena for at least five years, they become convinced that most of the phenomena they investigate are real. However, one must still approach the investigation with an open mind and try to find a rational explanation. This is especially true for those who investigate UFOs. Many skeptics would say, without very much evidence, that no form of paranormal phenomenon exists at all. They claim that the reports are a product of over-active imaginations. The bottom line is that serious researchers have to gather enough evidence to prove beyond a shadow of a doubt that these experiences exist. The evidence has to be solid enough to make the most hardened skeptic scratch his head and think twice. Logical explanations are constantly being proposed for inexplicable phenomena. For example, when thousands of people were seeing the UFOs in the Hudson River Valley of New York, the FAA came up with an explanation. They said that the sightings were caused by nothing more than a group of stunt pilots flying in "close military formation." This explanation did satisfy a certain percentage of the people who saw the UFO, but it was not taken seriously by those witnesses who had a close encounter with this unknown object.

It is interesting to note that the people who offered the explanation did not even see the UFO themselves. The people who did see the object were sure that it was something not of this world. Many of the witnesses who reported the UFO, and who were sure they had not seen planes, were professional people such as scientists, pilots, police officers, and engineers. These people would definitely be able to tell the difference between a plane and something strange, and they would surely think twice before they officially reported their sighting—unless they were sure that what they had seen could not be explained by conventional means.

A skeptic of the UFO phenomenon needs little or no evidence to make his point. However, a UFO researcher has the burden of proof. His evidence must be well-documented and undeniable if he is going to prove his case. This double standard is illustrated by an amusing incident that took place several years ago, during the investigation of a series of UFO sightings that took place in the southern Connecticut area during the summer of 1987.

During July of 1987, a large, triangular UFO was seen over the skies of Bridgeport, Connecticut at about ten at night. The object had rows of white and red lights, and was so huge that the witnesses who saw it claim it blocked out the entire sky. The object was seen by an estimated 3,000 people, and was also seen passing over the neighboring towns of Bristol, Westport, Fairfield, and Norwalk. The object was less than 1,000 feet in the air and made no sound at all. The people who saw it included police officers, and many others from all walks of life. All the witnesses agree that this unknown aircraft was at least the size of a football field, or larger. One witness stated, "I stood right under the thing and saw this black mass. It slowly moved overhead and made no sound. I looked up and noticed that the bottom had a number of circular holes. I saw a flashing white light in each. I also noted a network of what looked like some type of gridwork with tubes stretching across the bottom. It was made of a very dark, gun-gray material that did not seem to reflect the lights around it. The object continued moving to the northeast, and I soon lost it in the distance."

The report above is typical of over 150 that we received during that time. So many people saw this UFO that they began calling the local radio station in Bridgeport. The radio host at the time was Tiny Markel, and the format featured an open telephone line for listeners to discuss whatever was on their minds. Mr. Markel was very surprised when call after call came in, reporting the UFO. Mr. Markel told us later, "I could not believe it. When I first got the calls, I thought someone was putting me on. Then more people began to call in, all reporting the same thing. I knew that something extraordinary was being seen in the sky. Many well-educated people called. They identified themselves as doctors and others whose word I don't think I would question in a court of law. In my thirty years of broadcasting I never heard anything like it."

Mr. Markel told us how amazed he was, but then he said that someone called in later and "solved the mystery." Mr.

Markel said, "Toward the end of the show I received a call from a person who said that he got right under the alleged UFO and said it was a blimp." Phil then asked who the person was, because so many others with unquestionable credentials seemed to think that they had seen something out of the ordinary. Mr. Markel said, "Oh yeah, the mystery is solved. I asked the guy who he was and he said that his job was delivering fried chicken in a chicken suit in the Bridgeport area. All the time he was yelling like a chicken, but he seemed to know what he was talking about. As far as I am concerned he solved the mystery. He was sure it was a blimp, and that was good enough for me. I got on the radio later and told everyone that the UFO had been identified by a person who stood right under it and said it was just a blimp."

Dozens of people, ranging from police officers to scientists, called the station and reported a sighting of something strange. Then, one questionable person in a chicken suit called in and said it wasn't a UFO, it was a blimp. Who is believed? The man in the chicken suit. This is what we mean by the burden of proof. UFO researchers need an overwhelming amount of evidence to state their case, and often even that is not enough. Many people do not want to believe that there may be another intelligence out there that is greater than ours. Human beings would like to think that they are the most advanced form of life in the universe. This is why many people would accept any other explanation, since what the UFOs represent would take them out of their normal realm of security. UFOs, as well as many other forms of paranormal phenomena, seem to frighten people. We believe that the government took advantage of this fact when larger numbers of the public became interested in reading about close encounters with the unknown. At first, they made the subject look so ridiculous that people would not even take it seriously. Many refused to accept the idea of UFOs because they did not want to look like some kind of "nut." However, by the mid-eighties, many people from every country on Earth had had experiences that could not be denied. The government knew that there were just too many witnesses to call them all crazy, so they decided to try a new tactic to cover up paranormal occurrences, especially UFO sightings. They started spreading misinformation, horror stories of flesh-eating aliens and the bizarre experiments that they were doing on abducted humans. The stories that began to circulate through the media were so terrifying that people refused to believe them out of fear. A number of years ago a well-known writer told us, "If you want to cover up something, first you make it so ridiculous that people cannot believe it, and if that doesn't work, you make it so terrifying that people are afraid to believe it." This is what we believe has taken place in the study of UFOs.

How does one study this phenomenon, when you really don't know what to believe? The answer is simple. You have to start with the basics. Get the reports first-hand from the people who experience them. There are many groups that investigate UFO sightings. The two largest organizations are the Mutual UFO Network and the Center for UFO Studies. Although both of these groups have a large number of members and extensive case files, they really don't seem to understand the contact phenomena. Since there was no real research being done in this area, a Peekskill, New York attorney named

Peter Gersten decided to put together an organization that would explore the possibility that human beings were in contact with some type of non-human intelligence.

Mr. Gersten invited a number of well-known researchers of the paranormal to join his organization. During March of 1988, he arranged for the first meeting of his new organization, which he called "CONTACT." In some cases, members were flown out to New York from as far away as California to attend the first meeting, all at Mr. Gersten's expense. Some of the people who were asked to join, and who attended the first meeting, were Bud Hopkins, Phil Imbrogno, Patrick Huyghe, Tracy Torme, Peter Robbins, William Spaulding, Antonio Huneeus, and several others. Whitley Strieber, the author of *Communion,* was also asked to attend, but could not because of a conflicting work schedule at the time. Mr. Strieber was very interested in the organization and wanted to be kept informed of all its future activities. Gersten felt that Whitley's contribution to the research was important, since it was his book that inspired Mr. Gersten to create this organization.

At the first meeting of CONTACT, a great deal of attention was focused on trying to raise large sums of money so that people who had a contact experience could be brought to us from any part of the country. The money was also to be used to pay for the services of a number of specialists who might be called to help investigate a case. During the second day of the first meeting, just after lunch, Bud Hopkins made a strange comment to the group. He said that the number of people who have been abducted by the aliens is much greater than anyone realizes. He also said, "The reason why we are all here today and have this great interest in the phenomena is that most likely we all have had an abduction or a contact experience at some time in our life." Phil replied to Bud that he did not think he had been abducted. His interest in this type of phenomena most likely came from his background in astronomy. Bud did not reply directly, but indicated that everyone in the group should undergo regressive hypnosis to see if there was a UFO-related experience sometime in the past that triggered their great passion for investigating the phenomenon.

Peter Gersten then talked about organizing a free, all-day conference to focus on contact and abduction experiences and to introduce the new research group to the public. The conference was held at the Henry Wells Middle School in Brewster, New York during the last week in August, 1987. The middle school in Brewster was selected because it was the site of an earlier UFO conference that Mr. Gersten and Phil organized in 1984. This first conference had been a huge success. Over 1,200 people and fifty-two members of the media attended, including a representative of the *New York Times*. Brewster was also a hotbed for UFO sightings and close encounters. The details of this first conference can be found in *Night Siege*.

The speakers at the second conference included Peter Gersten, Whitley Strieber, Phil Imbrogno, Bud Hopkins, Peter Robbins, and a number of people who had had an abduction or a contact experience. The conference lasted twelve hours, and over 900 people showed up. Of that 900, over 300 filled out report forms describing their experiences. Many of the people who filled out the forms had had previous encounters with a UFO. These encounters then led to a contact experience. Many contactees were more than willing to talk at the conference. Also at the conference were thirty-four members of the media. The *New York Times* was represented once again, as were CNN and the major television networks and radio stations.

We obtained a lot of good data that day, but for some reason, several weeks after the conference, Peter Gersten dissolved CONTACT. To this day he has given no explanation of why the organization was terminated. There are all kinds of rumors, including speculation that he was under pressure from the government. We don't know how true this is, but at least two members of the organization claim that they were approached by federal agents just before the first meeting of CONTACT. These two members were told not to attend the meeting because the organization would be terminated before it could get started. This may be exactly what happened. CONTACT no longer exists, and Peter Gersten and many of its former members are no longer involved in UFO research.

CHAPTER TWELVE ...
THE GOVERNMENT CONNECTION

Shortly after CONTACT was dissolved, Phil received a call from Tracy Torme. Tracy is a very talented film writer who had written scripts for many TV series, including *Star Trek: The Next Generation.* Tracy, the son of singer Mel Torme, also wrote the movie script for *The Fire In The Sky,* a film about the abduction experience of Travis Walton. Tracy told Phil that LBS productions in Burbank, California, was putting together a UFO special which was going to be called *UFO COVER-UP LIVE.* It was to be a live show, during which the government was going to release information about the UFO phenomenon to the public for the first time. Tracy told Phil that Mike Farrell, known for his role in the TV show *M*A*S*H,* had agreed to host the show since he had a great interest in the UFO phenomenon. Mr. Farrell had read Phil's book, *Night Siege,* and thought that the sightings in the Hudson Valley were very important and should be included in the show. Tracy and some of the crew flew to New York City, where Phil and Peter Gersten met with him in the dining room of his hotel. At first Phil thought that this was just going to be another routine show about UFOs, but when Tracy began to describe the format both Phil and Peter got a very big surprise.

We were told that the show would be live, and that the government was going to allow them to show the alien contact that took place at Holloman Air Force Base. Holloman is located six miles southwest of Alamogordo, adjacent to White Sands National Monument, in the Tularosa Basin, and is the home of the 49th Tactical Fighter Wing. On July 16, 1945, the first atomic bomb was exploded in the northwest corner of the airfield bombing range, now called "Trinity Site." This military base has always been an area of high security, so it is understandable why this location was chosen for the first alien contact.

Representatives of military intelligence were also going to appear on the show and announce that UFOs are real, and that an alien intelligence had been visiting our planet for a very long time. Tracy told Phil that they considered his part in the program very important, and they hoped he would come to Washington when the air date arrived. Phil and Peter were asked not to talk about the format of the show, but you can imagine how difficult it was to keep that kind of information quiet. How would anyone feel if they were told that there was going to be an announcement in the near future that UFOs are real and they are the product of an alien intelligence? This is the kind of secret that is almost impossible to keep. In the weeks that followed we were quite excited about what was to take place, but we remained skeptical. It really didn't make sense to us. Why, after all the years of cover up, was the government finally going to release this information to the public? If they were going to do what Tracy told us, then it would be like dropping a bomb on the world. The effects might be devastating. Such knowledge of an alien intelligence could have severe repercussions on our economy, science, and religion. Every aspect of our culture would be changed—some for the better, some for the worse.

As the air date of the show drew nearer, Phil wondered why he hadn't been called, and began to inquire as to what was going on. He found out that the government backed out at the last moment, and was not going to turn over the Holloman film to the producers. As a result of this, Tracy and the rest of the production staff at LBS had to re-write the entire format of the show on a moment's notice. When *UFO COVER UP LIVE* was finally aired, it came across so disorganized and ridiculous that the show actually hurt, rather than helped, the study of UFOs. We are not sure what really took place, but it had something to do with a writer by the name of William Moore. It seems that Moore was responsible for changing the show's format. The program now centered on the testimony of two so-called government informants, who remained in the shadows and discussed things like how much the aliens enjoy strawberry ice cream. This made many of the viewers laugh at the show and made the study of the phenomenon look downright silly. In the months that followed, Moore publicly admitted that he was an informant for an unnamed intelligence organization in the government. Actor Mike Farrell was so discouraged by the program that he later announced that he would never do another television program that was concerned with the UFO phenomenon.

Perhaps this was the government's real intention for backing the show. They promised the producers all kinds of earth-shattering information, then pulled the rug out from under the program at the last moment, making it all fall apart. Whatever the reason behind this fiasco, the program made many people turn their backs and laugh, not only at UFO witnesses, but also at UFO researchers.

Despite the negative results from *UFO COVER UP LIVE,* we still received quite a few credible reports; by the end of 1990 our files contained hundreds of unexplained cases. Since a great deal of our research had been published in various magazines, letters came in from all over the world. These letters described encounters not only with UFOs, but also with some unknown intelligence that seems to be connected with the phenomenon. Interestingly, although these reports came from every part of the world, the encounters were all the same. People from all over our planet were experiencing the same thing! Most of these reports came from Europe, South America, the United States, Canada, Mexico, and Japan. We also received reports of several dozen cases from Australia. Sometimes we would get two or three letters from the same person, asking if we had received their first letter and why we had not responded. The truth of the matter was that in some cases we never received a first letter! This led us to suspect that someone out there was intercepting some of our mail—but for what reason? Our files have always been open to any qualified researcher, and most of our work has been published. If someone in the government was opening our mail, then they were wasting their time. All they had to do was pick up one of the UFO magazines, or any of several recent issues of *FATE.*

The number of letters that never arrived grew. Shortly thereafter, Phil received a call from a representative from the Air Force. The caller identified himself as Major Andrews and said that he was calling from Burlington, Massachusetts. Major Andrews' official title was the "Air Force representative to the FAA." Phil was quite surprised to get this call from a senior officer, since the subject of the conversation was UFOs. The major wanted to know how many reports we had collected of the sightings in the New York area. Phil told Major Andrews that he was researching the phenomenon and was convinced that it involved a real, unknown object, not some type of elaborate hoax. The major replied that the Air Force was very concerned about the UFO sightings in the New York area, although some of the reports could be attributed to a secret surveillance device which had been tested at high altitude over the east coast. The major seemed interested only in gathering information; at times it seemed as if he was reading his questions off some sort of form. There was no doubt in Phil's mind that he was merely collecting information for a higher authority, and that this particular officer knew very little about the UFO phenomenon.

Every time Phil tried to change the subject, the major always skillfully diverted the conversation back to his questions about the UFO. He was very interested in the sightings that took place over the Indian Point Nuclear Reactor in 1984 (this series of sightings is described in detail in *Night Siege*). He told Phil that the Air Force was very concerned about the increase of sightings in the area, and that they did not want a "UFO scare on their hands." He also said that the Air Force was investigating the sightings, and asked Phil if he would cooperate in an exchange of information. Phil agreed to cooperate as much as possible, providing the Air Force sent him sighting reports that they recently obtained in the Tri-State area. Once again the major agreed, but Phil was a little suspicious; he seemed almost too eager to cooperate. The conversation lasted about forty-five minutes. The major promised to send Phil a number of reports and documents that might help with our research. The conversation ended on a positive note. At no time was there any pressure or threats of any kind. The major just seemed to be doing his job. When he felt he had gotten all the information he needed, he ended the call.

Several weeks later we received a packet from the Air Force containing a number of reports. Although most of the documents did not contain earth-shattering information, a few were interesting. There were several reports from FAA air traffic control operators at the Islip, Long Island tracking station who had seen unknown targets on their screens. They asked the Air Force what they should do about UFO reports from private and commercial pilots. There was also a letter addressed to *Night Siege* co-author Bob Pratt from a woman in Tennessee, describing her close encounter with a triangle-shaped UFO. This sighting was also witnessed by law enforcement personnel in that area. Phil called Bob and was told that he had never received that letter, but Bob knew about the sighting because he wrote a story about it. How did this letter end up in the hands of the Air Force, and why did they give it to Phil when they knew that he had worked closely with Bob in the past? If we assume that the letter was not included with the documents on purpose, then the only other answer is that it was sent by mistake, and Phil was not supposed to receive it. This virtually proved that someone in the government was not only intercepting some of our mail, but that of other well-known UFO investigators as well.

It seems that the government has gone to great lengths to cover up major UFO incidents. One example of this is an interesting experience that took place during our research into a series of sightings in central and southern New York during 1987. The reports centered on the sighting of a giant, chevron-shaped UFO witnessed by hundreds of people. What took place after the sighting proved to us that some-one in a very powerful position was spending a great deal of money and resources to keep a lid on the UFO situation.

It was estimated that over 1,000 people saw this UFO as it hovered above the major highways of Putnam and Westch-ester Counties in New York. There was no doubt in the minds of the witnesses that what they saw was something very strange indeed. The UFO was reported to be larger than two football fields, and was seen over the course of several months during that last half of 1987. Several days after the sightings stopped, witnesses in that same area again began to report mysterious lights in the night sky. This time, howev-er, the lights turned out to be nothing more than a number of planes flying in a very tight "military" formation. There was no doubt that these lights were, in fact, conventional air-craft, since many highly trained people stood right under the them as they passed over their heads. Some of these people had seen the giant UFO on a previous date and also saw the planes. Many of these witnesses were able to identify the planes as planes, but they remained sure that what they had seen before could not be explained so easily. The planes appeared over and over again during the rest of 1987 and into the early months of 1988.

Plate 16. Planes in formation over the Hudson Valley Area. The planes were identified as O2As operated out of Stewart Airport by the CIA. Their purpose was to fake a UFO.

The planes were also observed by several witnesses using binoculars. They were able to draw the shapes of the aircraft that they saw. The drawings were all very similar, so we sent them to a couple of pilots that we know to try to determine the type of aircraft. One of our experts is an ex-military pilot, the other is an ex-commercial airline pilot who also used to fly missions for the CIA. Both of our pilot consultants agreed that the aircraft that were seen were of the O-2 type. The O-2 is a medium-duty airplane with a single or double engine. It is made by Cessna and is capable of long-range flights. This type of aircraft is used frequently by the CIA and the other intelligence organizations of the United States. The O-2 is used for surveillance missions and has very quiet, muffled engines. The newer models even have onboard flight computers, so formation flying can be achieved with little risk. We have received reports that as many as eight planes were seen flying together in a tight formation. Whoever the pilots were, they were very good. On several nights that they were seen the winds gusted to over twenty-five miles an hour, and they were still able to keep their formation.

We put together a research team and staked out the area for several weeks. On more than one occasion we saw the planes and were able to track them. There was no doubt about it, these pilots were very good, and the aircraft they flew made very little engine noise. The pilots seemed to be trying to fake a UFO. Many people felt that this was an attempt to discredit the real sightings that had taken place in the past. It's important to note that most of the sightings of the planes took place on Thursday nights, the official day of the week on which the Air Force flies night maneuvers. These mystery aircraft have also been reported everywhere else in the northeastern United States, shortly after there was a major UFO sighting.

The planes flew for about two hours and then landed—but where? They were seen circling Stormville Airport, located in Dutchess County, New York. The planes gave the impression that they were going to land, but did not. They then broke formation over the airport and headed west. Only on one occasion did we get a report of a plane landing at Stormville Airport, but no pilot got out. The plane stayed silent on the ground for several minutes, then took off and headed toward the northwest. As it flew into the night sky it never turned on its navigation lights. The witness who gave us this information lives very close to the airport landing field, and got a good look at the plane. She reported to us that the plane had no markings, and that the underside of the aircraft was painted flat black.

We finally tracked the planes to Stewart International Airport. Stewart is the site of an old Air Force Strategic Air Command (SAC) base. The base is now officially operated by the New York Air National Guard and the Marine Corps. The planes have been seen landing on the old SAC landing field, which is isolated from the main part of the airport. According to our research, this section of the base was supposed to have been closed down for the last twenty years.

We visited Stewart Airport on a number of occasions and found a large, isolated, fenced-off airfield far from the main landing strip. The area was closed off, and many signs indicated that it was a security area and that access was restricted. On the grounds were several buildings which looked like hangers. These buildings were large enough to house at least a dozen medium-sized planes. Although we were there for several hours, we saw no activity at all.

We then filed a freedom of information act request (FOIA) with the CIA to find out if they were using this area for some type of operation with small aircraft. After several weeks we received a lengthy letter telling us that the CIA was denying our request for information. They explained that if they acknowledged their presence at Stewart, it would endanger national security. The letter stated, "The Central Intelligence Agency cannot confirm or deny its activities at Stewart Airfield in Newburgh, New York. Any release of information about such alleged activities may in fact jeopardize the security of operatives and reveal the location of agents who provide information on matters of national security. Therefore, your request is denied for reasons that the information may be detrimental to the security of the United States and this office."

We feel that this letter is an admission that the CIA is at Stewart, and the planes do belong to them. It is also apparent that the pilots who are flying these planes are expertly trained military pilots with years of experience flying in a tight formation. What was going on in this restricted area? A short time later we were contacted by a member of the local Newburgh media. He told us of an experience he had while researching a news story at Stewart. This person told us that he found the restricted area on the base and was very curious as to what was going on there, since he had heard strange rumors for years.

As he started to walk through the restricted area, a jeep came racing out of nowhere. It screeched to a halt, and three military police (Air Force) got out of the jeep and took him by force to a building just inside the gate. He was pushed into a chair and was told to sit still and remain quiet. The room was very dimly lit; he could see no furniture besides several chairs and a table. After about fifteen minutes, two men dressed in dark suits entered the room and began to question him. One of the men had a computer print-out in his hand, which had his name on it. He told us, "It was scary. They had this computer sheet with all this information— they knew everything about me."

After one hour of being interrogated by the two men, one of them made a phone call. Our informant was taken outside and placed in a car, then driven to the public area of the airport, where a cab was waiting for him. One of the men told him not to say anything about the area he saw and what had just taken place. The man in black then said, "If you know what is good for you, you will forget this entire incident." This person remains fearful that the men who questioned him are still keeping an eye on him. He felt that they were from the CIA, or another branch of military intelligence.

During our investigation of this restricted area we found out that the base now harbors several large, C-5A Galaxy transport jets. This type of aircraft is the largest cargo jet used by the United States Air Force. We found out that a number of these cargo jets had been seen landing on the restricted airfield, and had been doing so for several years. We also discovered, through a document search, that the New York Air National Guard is no longer officially running the unrestricted area at Stewart. Since 1973, the base has been under the command of the Navy and the Marines. Once again the connection was made between Naval Intelligence and the UFOs.

Our research showed that the Department of Agriculture was also using a section of the restricted area as a holding place for animals. The information that we obtained indicated that a considerable number of cattle had been shipped to this location between 1984 and 1986. When we called the USDA at the site, a secretary told us that there had been so many shipments of cattle to that location, we would have to be more specific. We then asked to see all the documents of cattle shipments from 1982 through 1989, and were told that a request would have to be filed through the proper channels. In the weeks that followed we filed several Freedom of Information Act requests. After several months we still had received no answer. We contacted the USDA once again, and were told that our request had not arrived in time. All documents of that nature had been destroyed or

Plate 17. Several C-5As sitting on an isolated section of the airfield at Stewart Airport in Newburgh, New York.

erased from their main computer. The reason they gave was that, after a certain number of years, they delete a great number of records to "save space." We found this answer unacceptable, but later an inside informer at the base confirmed that the documents involving the cattle shipments to Stewart Air Base had been destroyed. We feel that our inquiries were delayed on purpose, so that the tracks of what was going on there could remain hidden.

What was the connection between the cattle and UFOs? Some researchers have made a connection between the bizarre cattle mutilations in the southwest and the UFO phenomenon. Some believe that the alien intelligence needs certain parts of the cattle to survive. Perhaps our government was trading large numbers of cattle for something that they wanted from the aliens? Perhaps they were using Stewart as a holding and distribution point? We did not know for sure, but the small aircraft that were trying to fake the UFO definitely were military and came from Stewart. This was confirmed in 1992, when we received a phone call from an individual who claimed to be one of the pilots who flew in that formation. Although the caller did not want to be taped, a brief account of his phone conversation with us is recreated below. The caller was a retired captain for American Airlines who also worked as a CIA operative. His job was to pilot aircraft for a variety of missions.

"Mr. Imbrogno, I was one of the pilots who flew in formation over the Hudson Valley. Although I am retired now, I do not want my name used, because I might be violating some national security clause. I was called by the chief of operations for the CIA in the northeast to fly a number of night formation flying missions out of the old SAC field at Stewart Air Base. There were five other pilots besides myself, all of us with about the same background. We were told to fly in formation around the Hudson Valley at an altitude of 5,000 feet at about 150 knots, which is very slow for formation flying. The aircraft we were using was the O-2A, which has a flight computer and a muffled engine. This aircraft is capable of long range and great stability. We were told that this was just a test flight to check the effectiveness of the new computer during very close formation, flying in windy conditions. I questioned this because the planes were equipped with unconventional lighting, and we were flying over a heavily populated area. We would fly over most of southern New York and some of Connecticut, then head north up to Cape Cod. We then swung around to the south and headed back to Stewart for a debriefing. I questioned these flights since it seemed that we were putting on a show for the people below. We were instructed to turn our lights on and off, and turn on the brighter, multicolored lights that were added to each aircraft. I really feel that the people who saw us from the ground could have mistaken us for a UFO. I know we are not responsible for all the reports because I saw this object myself, back in 1982, and it sure wasn't a formation of planes."

At this point the caller gave Phil further information about certain CIA operations at Stewart. The caller made Phil promise not to reveal the last bit of information, but we can tell you that it had something to do with the Iran-Contra incident. It is a very rare event when government agents interact with UFO and paranormal researchers, but in our case we feel that there was enough evidence to point to a very strong government connection.

CHAPTER THIRTEEN

THE SEARCH FOR ANSWERS

I t is not a common occurrence for UFO investigators to see an actual UFO, but with all of our research and the activity that was taking place around us, it was only a matter of time before we got our own view of this phenomenon. We knew that the majority of the sightings took place around magnetic anomalies, and that they were numerous just after the new and full moons. Our research showed that most of the sightings took place between the hours of 8:00 and 11:00 P.M.; however, most contact cases took place around 3:00 A.M. Although it was highly unlikely that we would experience contact with an alien intelligence, we were hoping to at least have a sighting of the strange aerial visitor that had been seen in the skies of New England for the past fifteen years. With all the available data, we tried to predict the next appearance of the UFO.

We had literally thousands of reports stored on computer disc, and it took a great deal of time to look for some type of pattern. If we discovered a pattern, then perhaps we could be in the vicinity when the next "window" opened. Our study indicated that the majority of the reports took place on Tuesday and Thursday nights. We really don't think that the alien intelligence cared about the day of the week, but their activities might be so highly structured and organized that they might show some type of repeating pattern when compared to our calendar.

The center of the UFO activity was located in Kent Cliffs, New York. Interstate Highway 84 seemed to run right through the area. Over the past several years, the pattern of sightings had changed, a fact that was evident when we analyzed the final computer printouts. The pattern of the sightings did not seem to be very complex. On certain days of the month, the UFO would appear in one location at a certain time, then disappear not far from the area in which it had first appeared. After hours of analyzing the data that showed the movement of the UFO, Phil was able to come up with a a date, time, and place for the next UFO sighting: October 29, 1987, at about 8:20 P.M. in Kent Cliffs and Brewster in Putnam County, New York. This information was obtained on October 15, so we had plenty of time to prepare. Although we didn't expect much of anything to happen, we put together a team of researchers so that if something did show up, we would be able to document the event.

We prepared four cars. Each carried two passengers and binoculars, and two of them were equipped with photographic equipment. All of the cars kept in contact with two-way radios. Police scanners were used so that we could listen to local and state police, who were usually the first to receive UFO reports. We decided to use I-84 as the center of our operation, and spaced the cars about two miles apart. Phil had a feeling that the rest stop near Stormville, New York, might be a good place to send one car to park. The rest stop was at a high elevation, with an excellent, unobstructed view of the surrounding area. Another reason we selected this location was that, according to our computer study, the UFO had a 42% chance of showing up within two miles of the little town of Stormville.

Our research team started driving westbound on I-84, and by 8:10 P.M. we were less than five miles from the suspected target area. Although the weather was clear and dry, it was somewhat cold and windy, a typical New England autumn night. We, Phil and Marianne, were in the second car in the caravan. As we continued to drive we all tried to stay in radio communication, but within one mile of the Stormville rest stop we lost contact with our lead car, driven by UFO researcher Chris Clark. As we approached the turnoff to the rest stop we saw Chris' car pulled over to the shoulder of the highway. The reason we had lost contact was because he was out of his car, staring at the sky.

At first, we could not see what he was looking at, because a small hill was blocking our view. We pulled alongside his car. Chris pointed to the sky and yelled, "They just appeared out of nowhere! They did a sort of dance in the sky, then joined together." We looked and saw a group of white lights no more than a mile away, very low in the sky. Phil went back to the car and got on the radio to inform the others that we were looking at something strange in the sky. He then instructed the other cars to stop where they were, pull over to the side of the road, and get out and watch the northwestern section of the sky, because the lights were heading in their direction. This would allow each team member to get ready to observe the object that had caught us by surprise.

As we continued to watch the lights they got closer and closer. They no longer appeared white; now they appeared to be a very light yellow. We could distinctly count eight very bright lights heading straight in our direction. From our vantage point the lights seemed to be in a straight line; there was no doubt that they were attached to some solid object. The object moved much too slowly to be a plane. It was huge and there was no sound at all. Although it was very windy that night, the UFO seemed unaffected by the wind. It was now less that a half mile away from us, and about fifty degrees above the horizon. Phil later calculated that, at its closest point to us, the UFO was less than 800 feet above the ground and its size was at least that of a 747!

As we watched the lights draw closer, we still heard no sound. It was very strange, almost unnerving to see an object of this size move so slowly without making any engine noise at all. Then, the object shifted gracefully sideways and began heading due east. At no time did we see any physical structure connecting the lights, but they moved so smoothly and in such perfect unison that we could not imagine them being separate objects. We could now see the back of the object. The lights appeared to be arranged in a sort of boomerang shape. More lights were visible from the back view. We counted at least eighteen various colors. The object displayed the purest reds, greens, blues, and yellows that we had ever seen. The center of the immediate back seemed to be made up of mostly red lights; it was such a beautiful sight that it looked like a Christmas tree in the sky.

Phil then got back on the radio and called to Fred Dennis in the last car, about a mile east of our position. Phil said, "Fred, it's heading in your direction." At that time we lost sight of the object as it moved behind a hill. We continued to radio to Fred, telling him that he should be seeing the object in a few seconds. Fred got out of his car with his binoculars and starting looking all around the sky, but saw nothing. He then saw a small plane at high altitude and said, "What is going on? Is this what they're seeing? There's nothing in the sky but a plane." He got back on his radio and told us that there is nothing in the sky. Then there was silence. About twenty seconds later, Fred got back on his radio and yelled, "I see it, I see it, it's huge!" While Fred was scanning the skies looking for the object it was still behind the hill. Since it was moving so slowly it took longer than we thought it would to reach his position. Fred observed the object, and he later told us that the UFO spilled out of the field of view of his binoculars. He was using wide angle binoculars, so this would make the UFO of enormous size.

The UFO was witnessed by everyone who was with us that night. One member of our team, who was in the third car, was an ex-New York State Trooper. He reported to us that he observed the object with high-powered binoculars as it passed right over his car. He said that he saw, "a number of lights that were attached to some type of smooth, dark-gray structure."

The UFO then picked up speed and continued to move east to the town of Brewster, New York, and finally to Danbury, Connecticut. We were still on the west side of the highway. To follow the object we had to get off at the closest exit, then get back on the Interstate heading east. We drove for about three minutes and then saw the object once again. This time it was heading west—the direction opposite to which we were travelling! We stopped our cars and watched the UFO drift slowly just above the hills at an estimated distance of a mile or so from the highway. We watched it for several minutes as it continued to move toward the west. We saw a multitude of red lights, which made up the back of the object. As we watched, all of the lights on the object went out. The UFO was gone. The time was 9:05 P.M. This was the last time we saw the object that night.

We were all quite excited by what we had seen. We met off the highway on a side road, to compare observations while the event was still fresh in our minds. At the time of the sighting, other cars also pulled over to the shoulder of the highway, and people got out to observe the object. We heard truck drivers talking about the UFO on their citizen band radios. We received many reports from people who saw the object that night in Danbury, Connecticut. All agreed that it was as large as a 747, and that it hovered above a main road, no more than one thousand feet in the air. One couple told us that, as it hovered above their car, the UFO started to descend rather quickly. This frightened them, but much to their relief it once again started to gain altitude, and began heading west. It is most unfortunate we did not have a video camera with us that night. All we had were still cameras, and we were disappointed in the way the pictures came out.

What was more important was the fact that we were able to predict when the UFO would appear. Phil predicted the time and location almost exactly. Several weeks later, when we tried to predict another sighting, nothing was seen. We were never able to predict another sighting of the UFO. Was the first time a coincidence? Or did it take all those years of research and countless case files just to predict that one event? It seems that the pattern of the appearance of the UFO could be more complex than we originally thought. Some members of our team believe that the sighting was not an accident, that the alien intelligence knew exactly what we were doing and staged the entire sighting for our benefit. If this is true, that would mean that some members of our team experienced some type of contact.

Although our sighting may have been just a coincidence, the computer helped us analyze the available data. Personal computers have been a great asset to many fields of scientific research, and the investigation of the UFO phenomenon is no exception. The results of a computer study of this most perplexing phenomenon appear on the following pages. This study represents the last ten years of our research. We must mention that some of the missing information was obtained from the Mutual UFO Network, the Center For UFO Studies, and the research being done by Dr. Willy Smith with the UFOCAT computer system. We also give special thanks to Bob Pratt, who has worked with us for many years investigating the reports. Bob is a true pioneer in this field, and has researched UFO incidents throughout the western hemisphere.

Distribution of World UFO Reports

Based on 3,160 reports

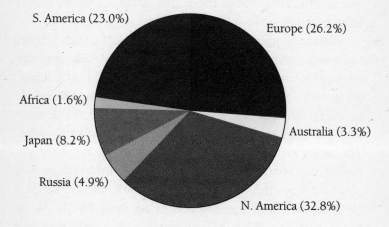

S. America (23.0%)

Europe (26.2%)

Africa (1.6%)

Australia (3.3%)

Japan (8.2%)

Russia (4.9%)

N. America (32.8%)

Chart 1. The distribution of World UFO reports. This pie graph shows the major areas of the world from which we received the most UFO reports. Although we feel that Russia should have a higher percentage than is shown here, it is still very difficult to get information from that country. Similarly, we do not mean to imply that sightings are not being reported in India, Thailand, or the rest of the near and far east. It is just that reports from these countries rarely reach researchers in North America.

Number of Witnesses to a UFO Event

Based on 4,139 witnesses in New England

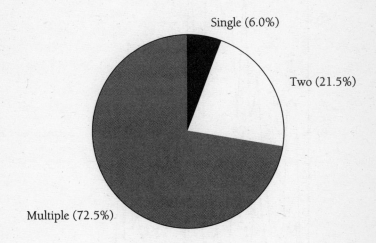

Single (6.0%)

Two (21.5%)

Multiple (72.5%)

Chart 2. This pie graph shows the number of witnesses to a sighting. It is a common misconception that only one person sees a UFO, and that no on else can verify the story. In this study we found that most cases reported to us involved multiple witnesses.

UFO Reports by Sex and Age

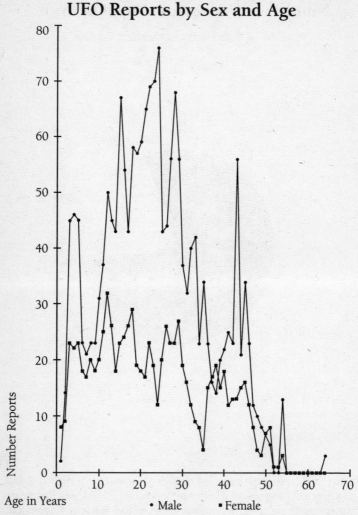

Chart 3. This line graph shows the age and sex of the people who report UFOs. This graph represents general sightings and close encounters of the first kind. In this case, most of the reports we received were from men between the ages of 15 and 30.

UFO Reports by Month

Based on 3,432 reports

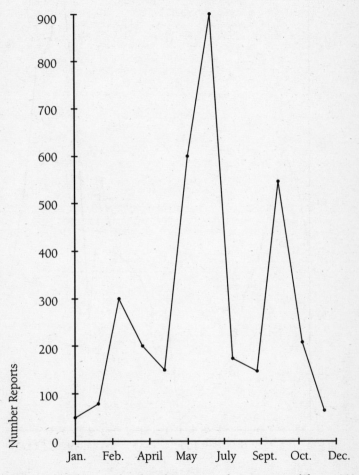

Chart 4. This line graph is based on reports that we received from 1983 through 1994. The study shows that the majority of sightings took place in June and July, with a smaller peak occurring in October.

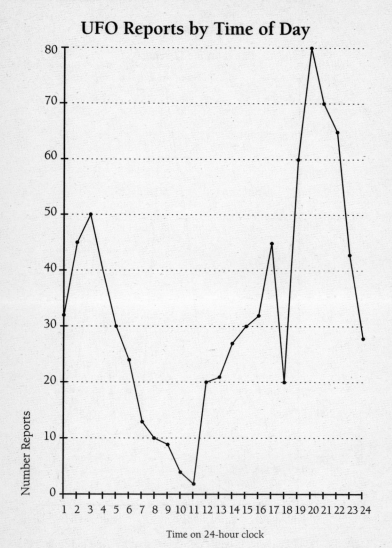

UFO Reports by Time of Day

Chart 5. This chart represents the time of day of UFO sightings. Note that this study represents only general sightings, which include nocturnal lights, daylight discs, and close encounters of the first kind.

High Strangeness Reports by Time of Day

Based on 120 cases

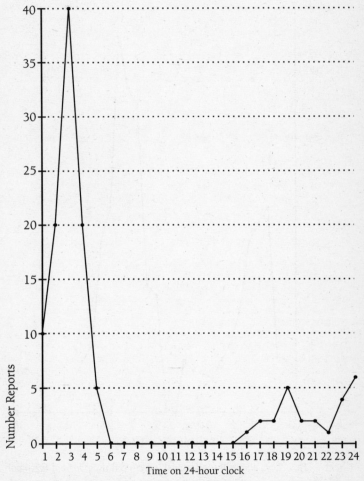

Chart 6. This line graph shows the time of day when most cases of High Strangeness take place. These cases include abductions, entity communication, and other forms of contact, especially close encounters of the third kind. Most of the cases take place between two and four in the morning.

UFO Reports by Moon Phase

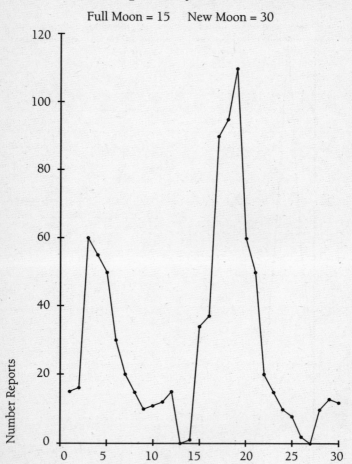

Full Moon = 15   New Moon = 30

Chart 7. This chart shows the relationship between the phase of the moon and UFO reports. The phase of the moon is given as "age." 30–0 represents the new moon, while 14–15 indicates the full moon. Notice that the majority of reports take place several days after new and full moon, with a large peak just after full.

Site Condition CE-II Cases

Based on 47 trace cases

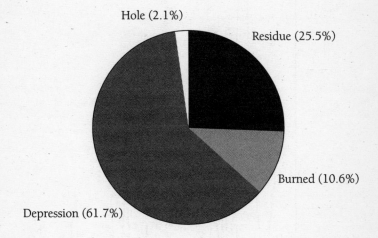

Hole (2.1%)

Residue (25.5%)

Burned (10.6%)

Depression (61.7%)

Chart 8. This pie graph shows the site condition of 47 trace cases that we investigated. In a trace case, the object leaves some kind of physical evidence that it was there. This type of case is also called a close encounter of the second kind. In the majority of cases we found that the grass or other vegetation was pressed down. In the 1950s these areas were called "saucer nests." They also resemble some of the early crop circles. In many cases we found a residue. On several occasions we had this residue analyzed; the results showed high concentrations of magnesium and potassium oxide.

Abduction Reports by Sex and Age

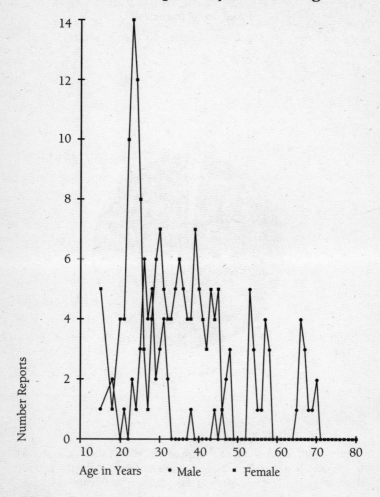

Chart 9. This line graph shows the number of reported abductions by sex and age. There is no doubt that women between the ages of 25 and 30 represent the largest number of abduction cases.

CHAPTER FOURTEEN

CONCLUSIONS

Many more cases remain for us to investigate. Perhaps one of them will have the answers that we are looking for. Recently, we were contacted by a young man who lives in Kentucky. He was desperate to talk with us, and even offered to come up to Connecticut so that he could tell us about his experiences. This young man claimed that he was abducted by the gray-skinned aliens on a number of occasions, and taken into a huge examination room aboard some type of ship. Although this case sounded like a typical abduction, it had a somewhat strange twist to it. The gray beings stood in the distance, while smaller beings in robes came around him and performed the actual abduction. He described these small hooded beings as having blue skin, but he could not make out their faces. He did notice that they had glowing red eyes, and three long, thick fingers on each hand. The last thing he remembered was being dragged by the hooded entities in the direction of the "grays," who seemed to be waiting for him. He then woke up in the morning feeling very dazed, with a bad headache. Many times, after an abduction, he has found strange cuts and scars on his body that weren't there the day before. He does not know what these creatures want from him, but they have been coming into his home and taking him this way for as long as he can remember.

There are several reports in which this small, hooded being has been seen, but the cases are very rare. Travis Walton (*The Fire In The Sky*) claimed that he saw beings of this type. Also, these hooded creatures have been reported around the location of Reservoir Road in Southeast, New York. Two people claim that, while walking on this road one night, several of these hooded beings came out of a rocky hill, walked down to the road, and approached them. The creatures, which were only about four feet tall, circled the two witnesses and tried to drag them back into the side of the hill. Terrified, the witnesses finally broke free and began to run. One of the witnesses looked back, and saw the creatures walk back up the hill and disappear into the rock. They reported that the beings were able to move through the rock as if it wasn't there. Did they create some type of "window" to return to their world? It is interesting to note that the hill and outcrop of rock where these creatures have been seen is less than ten feet from the largest natural magnetic anomaly in Putnam County, New York.

Cases of contact are increasing in number around the world, yet the scientific world turns a deaf ear to it all. There are thousands, perhaps millions, of people on our planet who are trying to understand the contact experiences that they are having. These people are sometimes very desperate to seek out researchers like us with the hope of getting help. One of the many problems facing UFOlogy, is that the major organizations do not work together—they actually compete with each other. There are also many so-called investigators who should not be involved in this research, because they do more harm than good.

We recently found a connection between blood type and people who have contact experiences. From our preliminary research, it seems that a very high percentage of those who have had multiple experiences have B-negative blood. What the connection is between the UFO intelligence and human blood type is not known for sure, but some feel that this very rare blood type was engineered by the aliens. If this is so, people with B-negative blood may in fact be off-shoots of the hybrid race that the aliens are trying to create. Perhaps in years to come we will be able to publish something definite on this subject.

Our research has been direct; we were personally involved in many of the case studies. We are not armchair investigators—we go directly out in the field and gather first-hand information. It took almost ten years to gather the data and and conduct the research for this book. We feel that we have presented enough evidence to prove that the contact experience is real, and we invite professionals from all fields to join us in our research.

We would also like to hear from our readers. If you have had any kind of paranormal experience, feel free to write to us at PO Box 4218, Greenwich, CT 06831. We are especially interested in photographs, tape recordings, or videos of UFOs or other forms of paranormal phenomena. Until our next book, we ask you to WATCH THE SKIES.

Stay in Touch. . .

Llewellyn publishes hundreds of books on your favorite subjects. On the following pages you will find listed some books now available on related subjects. Your local bookstore stocks most of these and will stock new Llewellyn titles as they become available. We urge your patronage.

Order by Phone

Call toll-free within the U.S. and Canada, 1–800–THE MOON.
In Minnesota call (612) 291–1970.
We accept Visa, MasterCard, and American Express.

Order by Mail

Send the full price of your order (MN residents add 7% sales tax) in U.S. funds to:

Llewellyn Worldwide
P.O. Box 64383, Dept. K361–1
St. Paul, MN 55164–0383, U.S.A.

Postage and Handling

- $4.00 for orders $15.00 and under
- $5.00 for orders over $15.00
- No charge for orders over $100.00

We ship UPS in the continental United States. We cannot ship to P.O. boxes. Orders shipped to Alaska, Hawaii, Canada, Mexico, and Puerto Rico will be sent first-class mail.

International orders: Airmail—add freight equal to price of each book to the total price of order, plus $5.00 for each non-book item (audiotapes, etc.). Surface mail—add $1.00 per item. Allow 4–6 weeks delivery on all orders. Postage and handling rates subject to change.

Group Discounts

We offer a 20% quantity discount to group leaders or agents. You must order a minimum of 5 copies of the same book to get our special quantity price.

Free Catalog

Get a free copy of our color catalog, *New Worlds of Mind and Spirit*. Subscribe for just $10.00 in the United States and Canada ($20.00 overseas, first-class mail). Many bookstores carry *New Worlds*—ask for it.

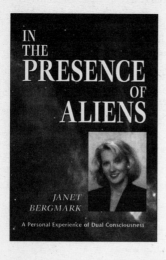

IN THE PRESENCE OF ALIENS

A Personal Experience of Dual Consciousness

Janet Bergmark

Strange beings remembered from childhood...ships in the sky over her Wisconsin farm... the feel of long, bony fingers on her flesh...and awakening to an alien presence that shares her existence. Science fiction? Not for Janet Bergmark, whose extraordinary, true-life account of the emotional, psychological and spiritual impact of alien contact poignantly captures the rare human experience of coming face-to-face with other sentient beings.

In the Presence of Aliens is the first book to speak candidly about the concept of a dual identity—human and alien; one body, two minds; two minds, one purpose—and its role in explaining why certain people are abducted by nonhuman life forms. Not only does this book explain how a dual identity is possible, it provides a first-person narrative of this unique and sometimes difficult relationship, including actual dialogue between human and alien.

1-56718-063-9, 6 x 9, 224 pp., softcover $12.95

STRANGE BUT TRUE

From the Files of FATE Magazine

Corrine Kenner & Craig Miller

Have you had a mystical experience? You're not alone. For almost 50 years, *FATE* readers have been reporting their encounters with the strange and unknown. In this collection, you'll meet loved ones who return from beyond the grave… mysterious voices warning of danger …guardian angels…and miraculous healings by benevolent forces. Every report is a first-hand account, complete with full details and vivid descriptions:

- *"Suddenly, a vision appeared at the foot of my bed. It was a young woman, wearing a sad expression on her strangely familiar face …"*

- *"Running across the clearing from one thickly wooded area to the other was a thin, hunched creature, covered with light gray hair …"*

- *"As I got closer to the white light, I heard a loud and forceful voice say, 'No!'…"*

- *"At that moment I whooshed back into my body and sat up …"*

Whether you're a true believer or a die-hard skeptic, you'll find *Strange but True* a book you can't put down.

1-56718-298-4, 256 pp., 5 ³⁄₁₆ x 8, softcover $9.95

ESP, WITCHES & UFOS

The Best of Hans Holzer, Book II

Edited by Raymond Buckland

In this exciting anthology, best-selling author and psychic investigator Hans Holzer explores true accounts of the strange and unknown: telepathy, psychic and reincarnation dreams, survival after death, psycho-ecstasy, unorthodox healings, Pagans and Witches, and Ufonauts. Included in this volume:

- Mrs. F. dreamed of a group of killers. Ten days later, the Sharon Tate murders occurred. Mrs. F. recognized the photo of Charles Manson as the man from her dream

- Several true accounts of miraculous healings achieved by unorthodox medical practitioners

- How the author sent a telepathic message to his friend via his friend's answering service

- The reasons why more and more people are turning to Witchcraft and Paganism as a way of life

- When UFOs land: physical evidence vs. cultists

These reports and many more will entertain and enlighten all readers intrigued by the mysteries of life ... and beyond!

0-87542-368-X, 304 pp., mass market   **$4.95**